Due North

Due North

James Viles

Photography by Adam Gibson

murdoch books

Sydney | London

Contents

Introduction

Premature Planning

I started planning this trip 23 years ago, without quite
knowing how or when it would play out, or even if it would
eventuate. Back then I was a young buck. I loved anything
that moved and I loved adventure.

At first the idea was to get some motorbikes and go around
Australia with some mates, just riding and camping. The
fact that we'd need to eat along the way, let alone fix
some piece of machinery, never really crossed our minds.
The trip was to start somewhere down south and end up
in Cape York, as far north as we could go. At sixteen or
seventeen years of age, what happened in between didn't
really matter - we just wanted to ride epic bikes through
epic conditions. As far as I can remember, I don't think the
months of preparation needed to pull off such an expedition,
or how hard it might be, ever occurred to us.

As the years went by, we all got busier and busier working
our day jobs, and talk of the trip tailed off. Until about
two years ago, that is, when I got the itch again, sparked
by various short trips to the Gulf of Carpentaria and the
vast wetlands east of Darwin. In fact, the whole bloody
country inspired me, reigniting the original idea - but
this time with a sense of purpose and curiosity.

I wanted to meet the people who grow and harvest some of
the produce I've been using at Biota for the past eight
years, to connect with them, and I wanted to understand
how the wild fish, animals and plants live in this country.
It's easy for cooks to get complacent, to get caught up
in all the bullshit that surrounds the industry. Don't get
me wrong, I still wanted an adventure - just something that
had been thought about first.

For me, the last few years have been about trying to find a way of disconnecting, of escaping all the commercialism. Chefs talk about connection, how our dishes connect with nature, but the real question should be how do we connect with nature? I mean, do we get out there and connect with nature, or are we all just waking up each day in the same place, doing the same thing... To connect with nature you need to listen, and you need to be in the middle of nowhere, with no lights, people, sounds, cars or shops to distract you, just natural beauty to take in.

Personally, I felt I needed to go off the grid, to 'go bush'. I needed to challenge myself, both mentally and physically. I wanted to sleep under the stars. I wanted less. But I also wanted more; I wanted to learn and develop a sense of belonging, something that would hopefully influence the next stage in my cooking. I wanted to see what this country is all about, and not through someone else's eyes, but through my own.

Tasmania

Wheel skids, car fridge, swag, tarp, computer gear,
phone chargers, cable ties, satellite phone, CB radio,
engine oil, tool kit, diesel cans x 2, ratchet straps
x 2, snatch strap, tyre pump, rope, knives, rifles,
ammo and case (lockable), clay thrower and clays,
fishing rod and tackle, torch and charger, drone,
soap, first aid kit - check.

Day 1

Packing

Tent, sleeping mat and sleeping bag, chairs (folding)
x 2, water bottles x 3, wetsuit, rain jacket. Fire-
lighters, small grill, tongs, gas cooker, jaffle iron,
plastic tub, whisk, bowls x 2, tea towels, cups,
plates, cutlery, coffee, beer, salt, oil, snacks.

What else? I'm sure we're missing shit...

Bin os + hunting kit
~~kit~~ are taking up
space →

It's about 11pm on a Saturday in late September, and I'm
in Bowral with Cameron Cansdell. A fellow chef and lover
of the outdoors, Cam has a restaurant called Bombini, at
Avoca Beach on the NSW Central Coast, and he was the chef
at my wedding. Over the years we've become good mates and
he's coming along for the initial leg of the trip, so he's
helping me pack. I collected the car from Land Rover head
office in Sydney earlier that day, and we're going through
everything in detail, over and over.

The whole trip will cover 13,000 kilometres and, along with
photographer Adam Gibson, I will essentially be living out
of this vehicle for a couple of months. We have our swags
and tents, but I have no idea where we'll be sleeping each
night, and I'm happy for it to be ad hoc - a quiet corner
of somebody's property, a nature strip or roadside campsite.

We have a massive YETI Tundra cooler to fit in, as well
as a fridge. We're struggling to squeeze it all in, so
we decide to strap as much on to the roof as possible...
At midnight we're still going - I just want to get this
finished. We need to be up early for the seven-hour drive
to Port Melbourne, where we'll board the *Spirit of Tasmania*
ferry to Devonport. It's 1am before we hit the sack. I'm
ruined and tired, but I can't sleep, can't stop worrying if
we've got everything covered, plus I'm bloody excited.

Day 2

Across Bass Strait: *Spirit of Tasmania*

Our day starts at about 6am. Both Cam and I are pumped
and we fly down the Hume Highway, stopping in a field
of vibrant yellow canola near Gundagai to water the
plants and stretch the legs. We reach Port Melbourne
three hours ahead of boarding time, but Cam and I soon
realise we have an issue: we have no way of brewing
coffee on the road. All we need is something small that
can go on the fire or stove. Cam's going through Google
and directing me around the city centre - it's ironic
that our first foray into hunting and gathering is in
Target for a coffee maker.

The trip ~~the trip~~ is getting real

Back at Port Melbourne, we need to line up early because we have a
small arsenal in the car: a Remington 243 rifle, with rounds of ammo,
and a 12g lever-action shotgun. One is for the fallow deer we hope to
hunt and eat along the way, the other is for wild ducks and waterfowl.
They do an inspection and insist that everything on the roof needs to be
packed inside the vehicle... Once this is done, a bloke takes the ammo
and rifles and locks them away in a cage. The quarantine guys actually
seemed more concerned about the fruit we had in the car than the guns -
this is Tassie, though!

When we finally get to drive on board, I get a message from Dave Moyle wanting to know if I'm in Tassie yet. Having lived and worked there for several years, Dave has helped me set up some amazing places to visit in the island state, and he's going to meet us in a few days' time on Flinders Island. 'Just boarding,' I tell him. 'Have fun on the ship, it's like a floating RSL,' he replies. He's right, this thing is massive. We park on the car deck and head upstairs. I'm thinking maybe an epic schnitty and, as for Cam, deep down I know he wants their finest sauv blanc by the glass (sorry, Cam). Instead we find microwaved pizzas (in fucking plastic). It's crook - and no, we don't eat. We settle for a beer and go to bed hungry.

Not ~~going~~ going
on this boat —
Looks like it has some
stories to tell though

Day 3

The northwest tip of the island: beef and octopus

We dock early next morning, by which time I'm ready to eat a body part. Cam jumps on to Google again and finds a little joint in downtown Devonport called Fundamental Espresso. The fact that espresso is spelt properly seems like a positive sign, so we drive straight there, to find unreal vinyl playing in the background. After a night on the *Spirit of Tassie* with its frozen pizzas, we need a dose of culture and good coffee. And by the look of their bagel menu, we're in for a tasty little treat - bloody epic bagels, I had two!

I text Adam, who is driving up from Hobart, to meet us here. He arrives with heaps of shit and camera gear, including a swag that could sleep about ten, so we spend the next half-hour working out how we're going to fit it all into the Land Rover.

It's mid-morning by the time we make our way towards
Stanley, in the northwestern tip of the island, to
meet a farming family whose passion for life and
nature inspires me. The fresh sea air, clean water
and high-quality pasture in this part of Tasmania
produces some of the best beef I've tasted in
Australia. The Cape Grim peninsula first came to
the attention of European settlers as early as 1798,
during Bass and Flinders' circumnavigation of
Tasmania. As most of this part of the island was
heavily forested, the pasture here offered precious
grazing land for settlers' sheep and cattle.

The Bruces began farming here in 1975, when David and Marie Bruce bought the Western Plains property, followed by Highfield in 1980. Four adjoining properties have since been added to their holding: The Oaks and Harman's Swamp in 1985, Morton's in 1996, and Glas Inis in 2013. The Bruces practise rotational grazing to ensure the cattle have access to clean fresh pasture every 2-4 days. John, David and Marie's son, explains that the exact timing of the rotations is determined by the leaf-emergence rate of the ryegrass, which is indicative of the strength of the rootstock. This varies across the year, depending on soil temperature and rainfall.

John Bruce and I discuss pastures and the fact that the Bruce family are not only beef farmers, but grass farmers

Talking deer heads
and white walls
with Iain Bruce,
John's son.

first night's dinner
with Cam in Stanley, Tas

John and his son, Iain, take us down to a special little part of
the property, where we set up camp - it's hidden away and there's
an old cabin looking out over Bass Strait where the family used to
camp out at night. Afterwards we head into Stanley for a quick look
around (and a couple of frothies at the Stanley Hotel) before we go
to meet Martin Hardy of T.O.P. Fish, who catch the octopus we use
at Biota. In the notoriously turbulent waters of Bass Strait they
set a total of 20,000 pots, lifting them when the weather permits.
They primarily land octopus, but also catch abalone and crayfish.
Martin shows us the facility, a processing area with large tanks
that hold octopus, plus crays and abalone when they're in season.
We take some octopus to cook for dinner over the fire, and Cam
spots a massive Southern cray he can't resist buying.

Back at Western Plains, we light a fire on the beach,
and while it gets going we spend the afternoon shooting
clays together and catching up... John and Iain are
dark horses when it comes to shooting - they turn out
to be better shots than Cam, Adam and I put together.

The key to cooking over any fire is good coals,
and when they're ready we set about getting dinner
happening: pasture-fed Cape Grim beef rib, octopus and
crayfish. We don't have an unlimited pantry, that's not
what this trip is about - it's about real ingredients
in their environment. There's something pretty special
about cooking beef on the land where it's been raised,
using octopus caught in the waters right in front of
you, and of course Cam's massive crayfish.

Fireside talks about
deer populations
in Tasmania.

We cook the beef rib, then leave it to rest. In the car, we've got some staples, such as butter, salt, pepper and a few sauces, but my idea is that we'll build up our supplies as we go from location to location. So for this first dinner, it's just chargrilled beef, crayfish split in half and cooked over the fire with butter and wild garlic, and seared octopus - simple, and yet amazing, when you consider that everything we're eating comes from within 10 kilometres of where we're sitting. The entire Bruce family, Adam, Cam and I sit by the fire and have dinner together.

Clay pigeon shooting on the beach

After a long day, we eventually crawl into our swags. But barely ten minutes later I hear a strange noise. Shining the light outside, I see there are at least twenty penguins waddling around our tents. For such unassuming birds, these little guys make some serious noise, and they go at it all night!

Day 4 ___

Launceston and Blessington: butter and a deer hunt

We pack up camp and have coffee with John and his wife, Angela, then John takes us to see his 'man cave', a sort of trophy room lined with the mounted heads of animals he and Iain have shot. John and Iain are keen hunters and conservationists, and today we are all heading to Blessington, on the other side of Launceston, in search of deer.

Fallow deer first arrived in Tasmania in the 1830s, with a herd being kept in the Van Diemen's Land Company's Highfield enclosure at Stanley from 1837 until at least 1851. Subsequently, releases took place on private properties across central Tasmania for many years, and by 1975 there were large herds in several regions. However, the harvesting of bucks and protection of does caused a surplus of females - and due to overcrowding, poor nutrition and a deficiency of mature stags, many of these females failed to breed.

In 1994, a deer biologist was engaged to work
with hunters, landowners and the government and
make some recommendations on how to manage the wild
deer population. These included a crop-protection
tag system, and educating hunters to harvest
antlerless deer, thus allowing young male deer
to reach maturity. Some areas have ongoing problems
with excessive numbers of deer, in part due to the
more widespread use of irrigation - this results
in lusher pastures and crops, which in turn attracts
the deer, and Tasmania's 5,000 licensed deer hunters
play a vital role in managing the population.

But first, on the way through Launceston, I want to stop
and see somebody I met a while ago, Olivia Morrison. Our
paths first crossed when I was working on a dining event
for the Melbourne Cup, based around Tasmanian ingredients,
and I loved her passion and drive for doing something she
believes in. She wasn't working in the food industry at
the time - she just loved good butter and saw a gap in the
market for real butter made by hand, using locally sourced
ingredients. She started making some of the best butter I've
tasted, out of her garage in Launceston and now, a few years
on, the Tasmanian Butter Company has expanded to bigger
premises that include an on-site bakery and café called
Bread & Butter, where we have a pit-stop for some lavishly
buttered scones.

Love a scone, actually –
with half an inch of
cold butter in it.

A beautiful buck.
It's nice to be lost
in the moment - this one's
just for watching.

When we arrive in Blessington, I notice the change in atmosphere. The altitude is higher here (about 600 metres above sea level) and the air is fresher; it reminds me of my home in the Southern Highlands. It's beautiful, a landscape of pine trees and big gums, my kind of place. We drive over and through creeks full of running water to reach a small hunting cabin. Built for cold nights in the Tassie highlands, the cabin is full of history - kitted out with equipment that's been left behind for the next time, it would surely have some stories to tell.

Discussing the best plan for fallow deer

We unpack and get organised, and we all talk about our gear. Very important in these situations, gear! Next we start to look at the weather, what the wind is doing, when the sun sets and rises. And finally the deer: follow deer, which is what we're hunting, bed down during the day and feed at night. Our plan is to catch them as they move into open pastures or paddocks to graze the adjacent woodland, feasting on trees crusted in lichen. Something about walking quietly through the tall timbers, stalking deer, makes your senses come alive - your eyesight becomes sharper, your hearing heightened.

We're out until about 11pm, taking a few shots at some deer on the edge of the scrub... When we miss, we decide to call it a night and head back to the cabin. With a fire going outside, we settle in for nightcaps and fireside chat.

Always practise patience

Day 5

The Derwent Valley and Hobart: adventures in fermentation

It's a very wet morning, so we decide to leave the Bruce family to go about their day and drive on towards Hobart. Adam the photographer suggests we take the scenic Highland Lakes Road, climbing about 500 metres into an eerie and dramatic landscape of denuded trees. We reach a sort of plateau before winding our way down through some magical landscapes to the Derwent Valley, where we're going to visit the Two Metre Tall brewery.

Quick tie down in
the freezing midlands
of Tasmania.

Back in 2004, Ash and Jane Huntington moved to
their 580-hectare farm from a vineyard in southern
France, chasing a dream of growing vines and making
wine here. However, when they discovered a rich
hop-growing history in the region, they decided on
a brewery instead. Since then Tasmanian ingredients
have become integral to the ales and cider they
ferment in their converted shearing shed, giving
them a sense of place and a connection to the land.

It's not called
'Two Metre Tall' for no
reason — Ash+Jane

Full of enthusiasm, they start talking about weeds, native ingredients, wild
fermentation and mash tuns. While Ash gets on with brewing a batch, Jane shows us
where the magic happens and we taste a few brews, including their classic Cleansing
Ale and a range of farmhouse ales. When Ash emerges from the shed, covered in the
day's work, he says 'G'day' and immediately starts talking about the variety of
grains and plants they use. It doesn't take me long to realise that any leaf
or grain they find is going to be fermented - these guys are so passionate about
their craft it's infectious.

I'm fascinated to learn more about the specific plants
he's working with, so Ash leads the way into a small
area of the shed that looks like a meth lab. With plants
everywhere and wild ferments bubbling away, it reminds me
of our workshop back at Biota. He starts by saying, 'I've
steeped this gear and got nothing. So it's almost a waste
of time. And then I thought, Aw, fuck it, I'll just put
a ferment through it and see what happens. And boom, it's
fuckin' tasty and totally off the hook. First you ferment
the natural oils that come out of the plants as they
are heated, and then you're starting to get all these
aromatics and you're just thinking, Oh my godfather,
OK, here we go.'

I could stay here for days talking wild plants, ferments
and gnarly flavour profiles... But we have to push on
to Hobart, where we need to put Cam on a plane back to
Sydney before we head off to meet another bloke who's
equally passionate about fermentation.

His arms are waving in all directions

Adam James first became interested in fermentation while travelling through Japan. He recalls the exact moment: in a tiny sake bar in Kyoto he was served a snack of fresh tofu topped with a fermented chilli paste called *kanzuri*. The intense, layered flavour and complexity struck such a chord that he dedicated his life to trying to recreate it.

Previously at Hobart's Tricycle Café, Adam has been dabbling in all things fermented for several years. Inevitably, hobby turned into obsession, and in 2016 he was awarded a Churchill Fellowship to undertake a 'fermentation world tour'. His research took him to Denmark, Italy, France, Georgia, China, Korea and Japan, where he studied fermentation techniques old and new. He is currently focusing on expanding his range of fermented condiments, combining seasonal produce with traditional methodologies.

I could happily settle in at Adam's house for
a while, especially as he has an epic vinyl
collection and we might even get to taste some
of the special miso he keeps hidden out the
back somewhere - he's always trying different
flavours and ingredients. However, we have to
go if we're to catch the last ferry for the
short hop across to Bruny Island.

Adam's ~~~~ abalone salt.
We take some of this with us,
might come in ~~~~ handy
Later.

It's an overcast evening, and as it looms out of the mist, Bruny has a certain calmness about it, a sense of being untouched. While Adam is taking some shots of the sun punching through the clouds, I stand there in the freezing night air and think about my kids at home. It's been less than a week and already I miss them.

Bruny Island is actually two land masses - North Bruny and South Bruny - joined by a sandy isthmus. We find a caravan park at Adventure Bay, on South Bruny, and we wheel in there and set up camp in about six minutes. We're getting good at this.

The place is deserted: it reminds me of the trailer-park scene in *Con Air*, but with gum trees. There's a caravan in the corner not far from us, and there's a massive barney going on inside. The night is dead-still, so you can hear every word... I guess it's all part of the experience. The weather is shit - cloudy, grey and wet - and what we really need is a hot shower. We find the coin-operated shower, a first for me. I love the idea of a coin-operated hot shower. But I drop my second dollar, and when I look down to where it landed I decide against foraging for it in the drain, so my shower is cut short. I got the important parts washed, though! We head to the pub you can't miss it, it's the only one on the island for some frothies and hit the sack.

Day 6

Bruny Island:
wakame-wrapped sea urchins

Next day we're up early to meet James Ashmore, the owner of Ashmores Southern Fish Markets, who supplies our restaurant with lots of seaweed and sea urchins and some southern calamari. I first met James a few years ago, when we talked about seaweed and his love of the water, and he's keen to show me the rich marine environment here.

It's about 7 in the morning, and Adam and I are hankering for a decent coffee. It's good to go on a trip with a bloke who drinks as much coffee as I do (before lunch). Hardly anything is open, so we end up in the ferry terminal, and the coffee is seriously crook - milky and warm. Not what I need before I jump into the brisk waters of the Southern Ocean...

At Dennes Point, we get changed into our wetsuits
and wait for James. Eventually he scoots round the corner
in a heavy-duty wetty, which makes me a little nervous.
He's a mad keen surfer as well, and he's already been
checking out the surf.

'What's the water temp, mate?' I ask.

'Oh, I think it's about 5-7 degrees,' he says.

Now if you ask me, that's fucking cold, even if
you do have some coverage on you.

wetsuit was
definitely
too thin

Looking back, this was the hardest morning on the trip for me, because it was so cold. I was really hoping that I wouldn't have to go in the water - I'll do anything on the land, but I'm not fond of going underwater.

So, naturally, James says, 'OK, we're going in. We're going to look for urchins and abalone, and see what seaweeds we can find.'

Adam manoeuvres the tinny into position and we jump into the water. It's like ice, and there's a strong current. James points out some of the seaweeds we use at the restaurant: frilly mekabu, ribbon-like kelp and the serrated fronds of wakame. It's amazing to see them in their natural habitat. When we buy the seaweed from him it's already been processed and packed in a beautiful little bag. It's a stunning product, really fresh, and contains different varieties depending on the time of year. All of them have distinct flavour profiles and textures, and some are used in cooking, while others are eaten raw. We pull up a selection of the seaweeds, so we can take a closer look at them. They appear totally different out of the water, with contrasting kinds of light on them.

Discussing seaweed with James →

All this time I'm swimming through 5-degree water in a 2mm surfing wetsuit that I usually do stand-up paddle boarding in. It's completely freezing, but put all that aside and you're swimming through this forest of seaweed that just keeps going and going. There must be 300 or 400 metres of it around the point, just waving in the water, with the sunlight starting to come through in the early morning.

Checking out the catch with James.

The whole time I'm thinking about sharks too, because James
had said there's been bull sharks around, and it's dark
still. Now I don't know if he's just said that to make me
shit my wetsuit - but I wouldn't be able to spot them anyway,
because with all the seaweed you can't see more than a metre
in front of you...

James goes down a lot deeper with a diving hookah on and
comes up with some stunning sea urchins. The waters here
are home to a mix of long-spined sea urchin, an introduced
species, and the native Tassie ones, which are whiter and
have shorter spines. The long-spine urchins are taking over,
so there is a program to catch and sell them, to allow stocks
of the native species to recover.

James introduced me
to this little number
a few years ago. I'm
going back for more.

James Ashmore,
'The old seadog'

This bloke lives for the water, and soon we're all sitting on the wharf, cracking open sea urchins. These are my favourite things - they remind me of ocean butter. Fresh sea urchins from the chilled Tasmanian waters, rolled in wakame plucked straight from the ocean. Hands down, this would have to be one of the best things I have ever eaten - a meal in itself, and our breakfast that day.

James keeps a short board in his tinny and is off to catch a surf break now, so we part ways. We drive over to the ferry terminal on Bruny (giving the coffee a miss this time) and head back to the mainland.

Day 7

Triabunna: scallops and mussels

We drive off the ferry and head north of Hobart to Spring Bay,
near Triabunna, where Phil Lamb grows the mussels we've been using
at Biota for almost five years.

On the way, we hit up the Triabunna fish and chip shop for some
deep-fried 'brown food'. Adam says we should get the scallops.
Now I'm thinking of the mainland chip-shop version of scallops -
battered potato slices, ideally dredged with chicken salt. But he
offers me one and it's an actual scallop. To be honest, I would
have preferred my type of scallop, which in Tassie is called a
potato cake, I'm told... WTF?

Love a rusty old brat! →

When we get to Spring Bay, Phil takes us
out to his marine farm near Maria Island.
The scenery is absolutely stunning, though
I imagine it can get pretty gnarly out here
on the water, especially in winter.

Phil tells me how it all began. They used to grow scallops, starting them off on the seabed, then dredging them up when they reached a certain size and putting them into lantern cages. But starfish ate too many of the young scallops - they tried all sorts of things, but in the end it just didn't work. It was very labour intensive, and every two years the wild fisheries would open and the price for scallops would plummet, so they gave that away.

However, all was not lost, as they discovered that the ropes holding the scallop cages were getting covered in mussel spat. The beard, or byssal thread, of the mussel, which is secreted by a gland near the foot of the mussel, enables them to hang on to the rope. The young mussels quickly grew, so they started selling those and just kind of transitioned into farming mussels. The mussel beds now span about 1,500 hectares, and it's the fast-flowing, deep water here that makes the mussels grow so well - it's unusual to have such powerful currents in a water depth of 25-35 metres. The mussels live on long ropes suspended vertically in the water, where they benefit from the flow of water carrying fresh nutrients to them, growing large and plump.

Algal blooms for growing oysters and mussels.

Phil ~~Lamb~~
Phil Lamb of
Spring Bay Mussels

We head back to Spring Bay, where Phil shows us his latest project, a room where they grow algae, which they then use to grow oysters from scratch. It looks like a scene from a sci-fi movie, with large plastic sacks full of living organisms. Through a carefully timed and exacting process, oyster seed stock is fed on the algae until the young oysters reach the size of a pinky-finger nail. They are then sold to oyster farmers all over the country, who grow them on to full size.

By now Adam and I are both hanging out for a coin shower and a frothy. Happily, the Triabunna tourist information centre has an amazing coin-operated shower, the best I've experienced to date - I'm becoming quite the expert now. Then it's off to the Triabunna pub to rip the scab off a cold one... Boags XXX, of course.

Day 8

Leap Farm and Maria Island:
goat's cheese and calamari

Our next stop is Leap Farm, Copping, a small pocket of
Tassie near Bream Creek, where I'm catching up with Iain
and Kate Field. They produce Tongola goat's cheese, which
we use at the restaurant for special dinners and events.

When we arrive, it's bloody mayhem... I have never seen so
many kids! Iain and Kate are both out on the farm: Iain is
flying a drone over the property to try and spot some stray
goats that have decided to go into someone else's paddock
for a quick arvo snack, and Kate is milking.

Iain and Kate at Tongola Cheese on Leap Farm in Copping

It's late arvo, so we head back to our camp
on top of the mountain overlooking Marion
Bay. This place is beautiful: fertile rolling
pastures, massive rock formations and coastal
air from a wild ocean. One of Adam's mates
who lives nearby drives up the mountain to say
g'day, really nice bloke, and we all sit by the
fire and have a few tinnies.

The ribbons for
lost kids.

Suddenly I start to feel pretty average. Now I never get
sick, I have iron guts, but I reckon that scallop from
Triabunna chip shop wanted out, and it was willing to take
the fastest route possible. It knocked me for six for
about three hours, then I was like a new man.

Kate's kids

Iain and Kate moved from the mainland to Leap Farm in the
height of winter 2012. They wanted to escape from the city and
seek a lifestyle with more simplicity and depth. The goats are
considered part of the family and are all individually named.
Every one of their goats is matched up, with coloured ribbons for
each mother and kid: blue goat, pink goat, green goat. It's quite
amazing to see fifty-plus kids find their mums in a paddock.

They tend their land according to robust organic and ecological
principles, sowing thirty-four species of meadow plants and
grasses to promote diversity. In the paddocks they have cattle
and goats, which are complementary species, grazers and browsers
respectively. They also have managed blackberry clumps to ensure
a good supply for the goats, who can't seem to get enough of it.

The simplicity of eggs, goat's cheese and toast

Iain and Kate pride themselves on taking a natural approach, following the natural lactation cycle of the goats and milking only once a day. Their milkers rest for three months while they're pregnant, and the kids stay with their mothers until weaning.

All their cheese is handmade on the farm, with deliberately gentle milk handling and processing practices in place. A big part of their philosophy - and something I particularly like - is that they understand seasonal variation in the milk and embrace it in their cheesemaking.

Every single day, Iain and Kate feed all the kids with a bottle - this is full on, it's relentless.

For us, just to be there for a few hours and see what happens in order to produce some of the country's best goat's cheese is unforgettable... not an easy gig.

We jump into the car and drive back up
to Triabunna wharf (bypassing the scene-of-
the-crime fish shop), where we're going to
meet a bloke by the name of Murray Knight
to try and catch some calamari. Murray
supplies the line-caught southern calamari
we use at Biota.

Southern calamari would have to be one
of my favourite ingredients, but I have
never done this before. Like all fishing,
it requires patience - and I have the
patience of a red-headed stepchild, so
I'm not going to last long. We boost out
there in his tinny, and the thing is
covered in squid ink, so I'm guessing
we're in with a chance.

After we've been out for about an hour, listening to a bunch of stories from Murray, I'm starting to wonder if we're going to catch anything. Suddenly, he spots another bloke on the water.

'Look at that maggot,' he says. 'I've been doing this for years and then these young blokes come in and just fish where I've been, but I have a secret spot up my sleeve.'

We head over to a sandbank off a rock ledge and throw a
jig in... Boom! A calamari chases the jig and takes it.
Now these things are predators, they attack. Murray pulls
it in and lands it on the deck, and it's massive. 'A male,'
he says, and two seconds later it shoots its load (of ink)
all over Adam. I reckon he's had that happen before, though,
as it doesn't seem to faze him too much, and we spend
another hour reeling in some more calamari.

We get back to shore covered in ink and keep heading north,
until Adam asks, 'Where are we staying, Viles?' I haven't
really thought about it and figure we'll just pull over
to the side of the road somewhere - everywhere up here is
stunning - but Adam thinks we might be able to stay on a
farm near Triabunna, owned by another of his mates. We stop
and say g'day, then head through the fields of Hereford
cattle, windows down in the car, smelling the salt air.
Adam says, 'Wait till you see this place, Vilesy...'

Southern calamari,
one of my favourite
ever ingredients.

We unpack the car, set up camp and go for a walk over a sand dune dotted with
samphire, warrigal greens, sea parsley and saltbush. The only tracks on it are those
of small animals and over the other side is a beach with white-as-white sand, orange
rock formations at its south end and crystal-clear water - it's bloody cold, though.
I have a few rigs in the car for salmon fishing, so we decide to walk around the
rocks and throw a few lures in... and just like that, we soon have a small salmon
and some parrot fish. That's dinner taken care of, so we head back to camp, open
up a few frothies and light a fire. To start with, we cook some vegetables with
eggs in a skillet over the fire and scatter over some goat's cheese from Leap Farm.
Then we throw the fish on the grillplate and sprinkle over some dried abalone. The
fish is unreal, the perfect meal. We hit the sack, and it's one of the best night's
sleep I've had on the trip so far.

A night in Bicheno hunting deer and eating goat curry

Day 9

Bicheno: another deer hunt

The next morning we're up early, ready for another go at deer hunting, this time near Bicheno, a small coastal town that backs on to a large national park. In town I look around for some ammo as I have run out. There's no sports store or ammo shop, but the local grocery store sells ammo, so you can buy your Winnie Blues, a case of tinnies, some Aussie-nan 'white bread' and some ammo all at once (only in Tassie).

We're fortunate enough to be staying in a cabin on the property where we'll be hunting. It's surrounded by dense woodland, and when we open the doors, there are deer antlers mounted on the walls, and shells and rifle parts lying around - a true hunter's cabin. We set off to scout out the best place to build a hide and settle on a small clearing in a field of fresh grass, building our hide down wind.

Adam and I go back to the cabin and put
dinner on. We have some goat meat from Leap
Farm in the car fridge, so I put on a goat
curry and leave it to slow-cook for a few
hours while we go hunting.

We sit in the hide for an uneventful two hours, then Adam spots a couple of fallow deer. Problem is they're about 500 metres away, too far for a clean shot - and by the time we decide to move closer to them it's already dark and visibility is poor. It's a shame, but I firmly believe that if the shot can't be a clean shot, it's not worth taking.

We head back to the cabin for our goat curry before hitting the hay.

Day 10

St Helens: in search of abalone

Tonight will be our last night on mainland Tassie
and we plan to stay in the Bay of Fires, which has
been on my wish list for a long time.

The drive to St Helens is majestic - we go through
a lot of small coastal communities, the kind of
places where you could just forget all your troubles
and live a simple life. We spend the morning in
St Helens having a look around, go for a drive to
the Bay of Fires to find a campsite, and lock one
in - it's magic, right on the water.

We're here to meet a guy called Dave Allen, who's super-
passionate about anything that comes from the ocean, and
has supplied seafood to some of Australia's top restaurants.
Adam and I head back into town to see him, but he's running
late so we decide to get some supplies to make a celebratory
dinner, in anticipation of actually catching some abalone.

'Adam's abs'
black-lip abalone
for dinner →

Black-lip abalone
from the Bay of fires

Eventually we find Dave. Almost a decade ago, he pioneered sea urchin processing in Tasmania, at Goshen, just inland from the Bay of Fires, and his enthusiasm for sea urchins is boundless. Soon we discover that we also both have a fondness for the southern mud (native) oyster.

Dave grew up in this area and knows it like the back of his hand. His seafood is great, and he really knows his stuff, but it can be a precarious way of making a living. He takes us a little further north for a dive. Adam goes in as well and comes up with a bag full of abalone - the smaller ones we put back, and the rest we keep. Dave comes back with us to share our last-night dinner.

Fireside abalone, cooked in
beer, garlic and butter.

Now abalone can be a real bitch to cook, especially if all you
have is a fire, but I think the best approach is to keep it
simple: just fire, abalone, garlic, butter and beer.

You need to beat the abalone with a rock or the back of a heavy
frying pan until a small crack appears on the top of the shell.
Place the abalone in the pan, cracked side down, then add a little
garlic and a dob of butter. Add enough beer to cover, as well as
a massive fistful of butter. Cook for about quarter of an hour,
then remove from the heat, cover the pan and leave it for half
to three-quarters of an hour. Go for a swim or something, or just
settle back with a few cold ones - the beer of choice for the
abalone is Boags XXX or Furphy.

Now cook up some linguine, slice the abalone super-thin and
then toss them and their juices through the pasta. So tasty -
especially if you're in the Bay of Fires, looking at one of
the prettiest sunsets imaginable.

ADAM GIBSON
Photographer

Being born in Tasmania, I was,
unbeknownst to me, delivered into
an isolated and distinctive part
of Australia. It was not until I
started to visit 'the mainland' as
a teenager that I realised just how
much the island state's separation
had shaped my outlook and character.
From this early connection to our
oceans, vast wilderness and people,
I realise now just how lucky I am
to call Australia my home.

These thoughts lead me to think
of a time before my family arrived
in Australia, the time of the
Aboriginal people and the precious
connection they have to the land we
share today - their sacred, ancient
connection. The more I travel across
Australia, the stronger my respect
for the knowledge and spirit of the
Aboriginal people grows.

Geographically and culturally,
Australia is a land of great
contrasts - and my life is built
around the pursuit of contrast,
of light and shadow, and of magic.

For me, travelling across the
country has given me the ability
to truly appreciate the spirit of
this place and its people, and the
incredible visual opportunities that
exist within it.

The chance to work with James
on this project was a once-in-a-
lifetime opportunity... however,
we're already planning our next
adventure, which is a testament to
what a brilliant experience this
book was to create. James and I
share a common view on many things
and working together on this book
was a fantastic, hilarious and
emotional trip that I will never
forget, and I am honoured to be
a part of it.

Flinders
Island

————————————————————————————————

Adam and I arrive on Flinders Island, a short
hop from Tasmania. 'Flinders', as the locals
call it, gets under your skin in the best way,
largely because of the people. I have been here
once before, for the Flinders Island Crayfish
Festival, an annual celebration of All Things
Flinders, where I first discovered some of the
island's amazing ingredients: Cape Barren goose,
muttonbird, wallaby, abalone, crayfish and,
of course, honey - the honey is off the hook.

Day 11

Quoin Farm and Killiecrankie:
burn-offs and burn-outs

Our flight lands at the southern end of the island, and
we unload a planeful of rifles and camping gear, then
reload it into a late 70s/early 80s Land Cruiser, a
beast of a thing, complete with original island rust.
(Our Discovery is travelling on the ferry with the
cattle and won't arrive until tomorrow.) We jump in
and drive to the bottle shop for a quick frothy - yes,
it is 10am on Flinders, but we were up very early.

We're heading north towards Killiecrankie, and on the
way we drive through the main town of Whitemark. I'm keen
to pick up a scallop or crayfish pie at the bakery, but
they're closed. Every time I've been to Flinders, locals
tell me I've got to have one, and every single time they're
closed. I'm beginning to think they don't exist!

We're going to see Jo and Tom Youl, who have been pivotal
in promoting local produce and encouraging tourism. At Quoin
Farm, the family property just outside Killiecrankie, they
run about 500 Angus cattle and aim to increase their herd,
as well as plant avocado trees and develop sustainable
accommodation and visitor experiences. Jo also has a food
business called A Taste of Flinders, with two venues on the
island: Taste cafe and The Flinders Wharf, a waterfront
complex that houses a restaurant, bar and providore, plus
the Furneaux whiskey distillery. They are a dynamic couple
with big plans.

Jo, Tom
+ Buddy

One of the challenging things about living on
Flinders is that it's like living 'with the family',
under the same roof for your whole life. It's a
small community, with a certain way of living, and
when people move here to try new ventures, locals
don't always accept that. As with all remote places,
there's a balance to be struck between bringing
in new business and tourism and keeping things
the same. There are often disagreements over both
business practices and farming practices, though
of course this can happen in all small communities.
To my mind, a positive attitude is essential, and
if new people are contributing to that, then it has
to be a good thing.

When we get to Quoin Farm, I ring Tom to find out
where he is, and he says, 'I'm just lighting a few
fires...' Soon we see a shitload of smoke, he's
doing a controlled burn. We get out of the car and
Tom hands me 'The Bug'. Now, this thing is probably
pretty dangerous in the wrong hands. Let's just
say I'm glad he gave it to me and not Adam! He's
always got this look in his eye, like he could cause
some mischief, and he was the back-seat naughty
boy the whole trip - we never let him anywhere near
the rifles. Tom points to a corner fenceline about
400 metres away and says, 'Walk that way and light
it up.' At first I thought he was joking. Was he
actually going to give me this thing to set fire to
40 acres of his land? Still, if he says so, count me
in. So I walk over to the fenceline with 'The Bug'
and I light shit up.

first time with
a bug! →

Three hours later, and it's amazing to see
how this burning off changes the landscape
and to discover why it is done. Every year,
before spring, the old foliage of the silver
tussock grass, which is unpalatable to
livestock, is burnt off to encourage the
tussock and other grasses to regenerate with
new growth and sweeter young leaves for the
cattle. And here's what I love about this
place: I have been on the island for barely
four hours and already I'm learning stuff.

never been asked
to burn 40 acres
before

Killiecrankie beach ↗
~~fun~~ + games
fun

'The Cray Shack'
— our humble abode →

We drive across to The Cray Shack in
Killiecrankie, where Tom and Jo are putting
us up for a few nights. After being in the
swags for over a week now, it's nice to have
a shower and a real bed. As dusk falls, we
head out onto the beach at low tide for some
fun in the sand: cue sand burn-outs and a
blast of fresh, salty air before we hit
the hay for the night...

Our not-so-shit view
from The Cray Shack.

Day 12

Big Dog Island:
muttonbirds and wallabies

The next morning, we set off to explore a little.
John Wells, a seasoned muttonbirder, takes us to the
sacred rookeries on Big Dog Island. The weather is
gnarly, it's bloody freezing and blowing an absolute
gale. I imagine Big Dog Island gets even more real
in winter.

Nesting in burrows on clifftops, the muttonbird,
or short-tailed shearwater, has been exploited
commercially since the early nineteenth century;
during World War II, the birds were canned and sold
in Britain as 'squab in aspic'. While there were no
controls in the early days, today the industry is
subject to stringent regulations, and current research
is monitoring the muttonbird population carefully, to
ensure that a proper ecological balance is maintained.

The sheds –
behind are the
sacred rookeries

John's interest in muttonbirding began in childhood, when relatives who were custodians of the rookeries brought muttonbirds and oil to sustain the family during the winter. He vividly remembers being given spoonfuls of the oil to alleviate cold symptoms, and he would hide any signs of being unwell to avoid its anchovy-like taste. More recently he has used the oil for treating various ailments, with impressive results, and has since launched Ocean Omegas to promote its potential health benefits. John is passionate about protecting muttonbirds - or *yolla* ('moonbirds') as he calls them - and the marine environment that sustains them, explaining that we are merely caretakers of the oceans for the generations that will follow us.

Muttonbirding is mostly the preserve of local Aborigines carrying on their traditional activity, and the season lasts from 17 March to 30 April each year. Young birds are harvested for their oil, which is rich in omega-3 fatty acids and minerals; their fat, which is sold to local dairy farmers for use as a feed supplement; their feathers and down, which are prized for upholstery; and their flesh, which is either eaten by the local Aboriginal community, or salt-cured and sold on the mainland. The place feels eerie and deserted, and the shacks the muttonbirders live in are little more than simple sheds. As we walk around I can't help but think about the history and significance of the place, and why such places are so important.

Hand plucking in the sheds

John Wells talks about muttonbirding and its important place in Indigenous culture.

I feel privileged to be here with John, yet I also feel a sense of disgrace about what's happened here in the past. He points me to a site I should visit back on Flinders, on the west coast of the island. Wybalenna tells the sad and disturbing story of Aborigines on Flinders Island, a story of maltreatment and misguided attempts to solve a problem, while actually exacerbating it. In 1834 a total of 134 Tasmanian Aborigines, believed at the time to be the last of their race, were isolated on the island in an attempt to 'civilise' them, and to protect them from the rape and murder inflicted on them by European settlers and sealers on the Tasmanian mainland. This was never going to work, not least because the soldiers and brutalised men charged with the task were, in fact, the problem. Stranded, and far away from their traditional lands, many of the Aborigines perished here. By 1847 the settlement at Wybalenna was considered a failure. The site was abandoned, and the 47 surviving Aborigines were moved to Oyster Cove, south of Hobart.

For a time, the remains of the settlement fell
into disrepair. Then the 1970s and 1980s saw a
bitter and protracted dispute, with Tasmanian
Aborigines asserting that the land should be
protected and the unmarked graves respected.
The site was finally returned to local Aborigines
by the Tasmanian Government under the Aboriginal
Lands Act of 1995. Now a National Trust site, the
small chapel here contains a number of Aboriginal
artefacts and some informative storyboards that
recount the history of the ill-fated settlement and
the lives of some of its most famous inhabitants,
including William Lanne and Truganini.

Later that afternoon we go hunting. I'm after wallaby to make a wallaby-tail ragu for a dinner we're putting on for some mates and locals tomorrow night. It shouldn't be too hard. Wallabies are considered a pest on Flinders - they are everywhere, and I mean everywhere. Although efforts have been made to control them by making their meat available commercially and farmers being given culling quotas, their sheer numbers are still an issue. We should be eating more of them... but tonight I only need two. We take them down with the .243 and then Tom shows me his skinning and cleaning technique. He says you really need to put your back into it: he cuts a slit along the stomach and then swings the whole wallaby over his shoulder. Gravity pulls all the entrails out for us, and we leave them there for other animals to eat - this is the most sustainable way to do it (or you might bury them for Mother Earth, depending on where you are).

Tom gives me a lesson in field dressing a wallaby, the _correct_ way that maintains the integrity of the meat.

We have Buddy, Tom's dog, with us... Buddy is waiting patiently for a leg - I don't think he's fussy, though. We take the wallabies back to the shack and break them down. My favourite part is the tail, especially for slow-cooking, but of course we're going to use the whole animal. We're making a real stockman's stew - a version of it is on the Biota menu for winter. In colonial times in Australia, stockmen would rarely eat their own livestock because they needed the sales. Instead they'd often shoot wallaby or roo to eat, cooking it with introduced ingredients they'd brought with them. We use the legs and tail, along with some pepper leaf we'd found in Tassie, a spoonful of Adam's miso and some wild garlic. Like oxtail, wallaby tail is quite fatty, so you don't need to add any extra fat to it. I leave the ragu to cook very slowly overnight, ready for our family meal the next day.

Tomorrow, I'll make flatbreads to go with it - just a simple dough made from flour, salt and a bit of yoghurt, left in the sun to ferment for the day, then flattened out and cooked right on the fire until blistered and slightly charred.

Wallaby prime-cuts I'm using the tail and legs in a ragu for tomorrow's dinner.

Wallaby butchery in play.

Wallaby-tail ragu,
wild garlic and
flatbreads cooked
over the coals.

Day 13

Stacky's Bight:
a wild goose chase and a wombat

Early the next morning I walk out onto the deck of the
shack, and I think to myself, this is it, this place is
magic. Why do we always want more? This is enough for
me right now. I could very happily wake to this scene
every day: the rocks, the white sands, the seashore
plants. I'm struck by the notion that we seem compelled
to want more than we need. We often feel lost and
desperately want connection, yet we don't quite know
how or where to get it. Well, maybe it's right under
our noses, maybe by removing the 'more' in life and
focusing on the 'less', we can all start to feel
connected again. This trip is starting to make sense,
it's starting to have a profound effect on me, or
maybe it's not the trip, it's just being surrounded
by nature and life taking on a slower more relaxed
pace... Whatever it is, spending time in such beautiful
landscapes and sharing meals around the fire is
working wonders.

Our plans for the day involve Cape Barren goose, a wild bird I first tasted last year at the island's Crayfish Festival. They're absolutely amazing birds: large and grey, delicious, and plentiful on Flinders. Given their breeding capacity and their impact on crops, seasonal hunting quotas are in place, and there's an argument to be made for marketing them as wild game birds - but they're damn hard to catch!

Last year I actually made schnitties with the breast meat: I coated them in beaten egg and a mix of corn-meal, millet seeds and breadcrumbs, then served them with chopped saltbush and other local wild plants. They were so tender and tasty, with a light gamey flavour. My heart is set on one of these birds, but after several hours of hiding in bushes and stalking them, we have no luck this time. The geese can be incredibly flighty, they move in large packs, and it takes just one to notice you - which I think only adds to the eating experience when you do finally nab one.

Wood duck, my ~~favorite~~ favourite ← to eat

Cape Barren goose schnitzel.

By now, Tom is looking tired, so we decide to scrap our wild goose chase. 'I'll take you fellas to a special spot,' he says. We drive the ute across the beach until we reach a small track... Buddy is still with us, he goes everywhere. In fact, I think Buddy is the one who knows where we're going - he's sitting next to me, panting heavily, full of anticipation. We park to one side of a small headland and walk around the corner to a small cove called Stacky's Bight.

We get up onto the headland area, which is really rugged and extreme, and I look down over an expanse of turquoise water. It's bright and clear, almost fluorescent, and on one side there's what looks like a massive skate ramp of rock, ultra-smooth, just going down into the water. I've never seen something this pretty, a white-sand bay enclosed by rocky cliffs, a hidden place with nobody in sight.

Anyway, Buddy has already taken off. He's in his element here and just loves it. I'm throwing the stick for Buddy and he's running up and down the beach, and there's this beautiful big archway, a natural rock formation, that perfectly frames the view out to sea and the Bass Strait. We didn't come here to get any food or ingredients, but just to look, and it's really nice of Tom to show us his secret spot, a place he and his family love and cherish. We could easily spend the whole afternoon here. These sorts of places, you don't even know they exist unless somebody like Tom takes you there. They touch you in a special way, because it's the first time and also maybe the last time you'll ever visit, and you know that while you're there.

As we drive back, we're all having a chat about dinner. We've got some local snapper and the wallaby ragu, to be eaten with flatbreads. Then Tom asks if I've ever eaten wombat. Now I've eaten a lot of things, but I've never eaten wombat before. However, from my reading, I know that the early settlers ate 'the keg on legs' because it was easy to hunt and cooked well in a campfire stew. Tom explains that he has a permit to shoot a certain amount of wombats each year on his property.

We don't go out actively looking for them, but they are
everywhere. Tom explains that a younger one is better, and
the next thing I know, Tom spots a young wombat shuffling
along at the side of the road. Tom takes the shot and ends
its life quickly and cleanly. Now I'm not too sure where
to start with this thing, but we remove its skin and vital
organs... not really any different to any other animal.
We let the meat set for a day and then Tom decides to cook
it slowly on a spit over the fire.

Some of Sophie's
~~to cut~~ garlic,
locally grown
on the island

Adam and I pick a few handfuls of saltbush, which grows in abundance on the island:
some goes through the ragu for its last minute of cooking, then I scatter some
raw on top to finish. I put all the food out for everyone: we have snapper cooked
over the fire, whiting cooked in butter flavoured with wild garlic gathered from
around the shack, the wallaby ragu with grilled flatbreads, and finally the wombat.
Tom brings in the whole wombat and cuts it up so we can all have a piece. I'm
curious to try it. After all, it's just another meat... Well, to be honest,
it makes me think there are good reasons why we don't eat wombat. It's pretty
lean and tastes very average to me - dry, dull and pale. But others, like young
Alice, are keen: given a leg to gnaw on, she pipes up with 'Daddy, I love wombat.
Can I have some more?'

Green-lip abalone
steamed in the shell
with wild garlic.

Epic green-lip abalone, caught by Adam Gibson

Day 14

To Trousers Point and back:
abalone and honey

As soon as we're awake, Adam and I head straight down
to Trousers Point to dive for green-lip abalone. Adam
pulls up some rippers. We have a few cheeky tins at
the beach and then take the abalone back to the shack,
ready for dinner later.

Soon we're off again, this time to meet John Siermicki,
who has been a beekeeper on the island for some fifteen
years. It's misty and cold as we drive through the
rolling hills where John has his hives. We arrive on
top of a windy yet protected peak, and John leads the
way through the trees, which are covered in white and
pale pink flowers. We enter a clearing full of beehives
and it's like being in another world: all I can smell
is honey and the heady perfume from the flowering
trees, and all I can hear is the surprisingly loud
buzzing of the bees.

Our mate
Grimmy in his
element

John has over 700 hives across Tassie and Flinders, and harvests between 10 and 12 tonnes of honey each year. Considering each bee makes about a teaspoon of honey in its entire lifetime, we're talking about a lot of bees. Flinders is renowned for the pollution-free winds that blow across Bass Strait, making for unusually pure honey, with a distinct flavour profile. In addition to his manuka honey, John also harvests meadow honey, from hives positioned to encourage the bees to forage among fields of dandelions.

John talks manuka

I ask John what the bees are feeding on, and he says
manuka. Now, I thought manuka was only found in New
Zealand, but John tells me that we actually have more
varieties of manuka (tea tree) here in Australia and
that there is a particularly high concentration of
them in Tasmania and on Flinders. I go over to pick
a flower and eat it - it's amazing, so sweet, fragrant
and crisp. John suits me up, then he tells me to place
my hand on top of one of the hives: it's so warm to the
touch, almost hot. I've always been fascinated by bees -
I firmly believe they are the world's best engineers,
and we have our own hives at Biota and Barn.

Later that afternoon, I'm in the kitchen back at the Youls'
place getting dinner ready, burners blazing away on the stove,
when I turn around for a moment. Something happens with the
gas and suddenly there's a noise like a bomb going off, so
bloody loud, and the oven door flies over and hits me in the
back... Tom rushes in, but is surprisingly unfazed - turns
out there's a bit of a tradition of chefs blowing shit up at
their place. Enter David Moyle. Now Dave's nickname is Diesel,
because one time he filled up a diesel car with unleaded petrol
and destroyed it. Tom and Jo keep a tally of which chefs have
fucked up what while staying at their place. Dave's first, and
I'm second, with the exploding oven scoring highly.

We improvise, cooking the abalone on a smaller burner, and then
all sit down together to big bowls of green-lip abalone cooked
in garlic and butter. I mean where else does this happen?

This is special. And bittersweet. It's our last supper on
Flinders; the next morning we need to leave for the mainland.

DAVID MOYLE
Chef and nature lover

I trained in an Italian restaurant in Melbourne, in a kitchen built into a double-fronted Victorian-era building. Under the guidance of a chef of German/Italian descent I learnt how to apply an Italian sensibility to ingredients derived from Europe but mostly produced locally. And I grew up in an Irish/English/Welsh family, in coastal western Victoria, not far from the UNESCO World Heritage Budj Bim site, which contains signs of early aquaculture and eel traps more than 6,500 years old, yet I only learnt of its existence two years ago.

Cooking is such a privilege, and it provides not only a living but also the opportunity to connect with so many people - customers, producers and contemporaries. We know so little of what came before, and gaining an insight into human diet and agriculture is possibly one of our most important pursuits for the future. I have become obsessed with the ethics and philosophy of what we eat, learning about production and cultivation, witnessing death. It's really heavy shit. Watching or participating in the slaughter of an animal is something I don't ever want to get used to. I still cry at the death of a goddamn cockroach.

For me, engaging with the wild food environment is not about sustainability, it is all about conservation. Your senses change when you are fishing in the sea or stalking in the forest. You become aware of everything around you: where the water is running, animal tracks, changes in wind direction. Sourcing food from these self-sustaining ecosystems is a privilege that has shifted my perspective.

James's approach to food has come through putting himself into these unfamiliar places. The food culture we apply is borrowed from other regions very different to this island. It's funny that we chase after authenticity, but have only touched the surface of what this land can sustain. In order for us to move forward, we need to acknowledge the past and how the land was used.

The time we live in is characterised by a disconnection from nature, and our food systems encourage a lack of awareness about its workings. To be in the wilderness reminds us that we are a part of nature, that we do not preside over it. We need to feel small to appreciate the world's enduring quality, to recognise how little it takes to affect it. Our impact may be significant, but ultimately we will be insignificant. These experiences are my motivation.

I have been lucky enough to join James out in nature several times, and every trip is special. You learn so much by removing yourself from the built environment techniques, methods and ethics - but the greatest skill honed from these times is observation. You listen and watch and smell and touch. It really draws you in and can be deeply moving. It is also the most fun I have ever had.

The Coorong
& Eyre Peninsula

————————————————————————————————————

After another trip on the good old *Spirit of Tasmania*,
we dock in Port Melbourne and set off towards Adelaide.
There we pick up my mate Ryan Kovacs (chef at Bertha's
Meats, back in Bowral) from the airport and do a quick
re-pack of the Discovery, tying everything down and filling
all the jerry cans - there are some pretty long stretches
in the Outback where there's nowhere to get fuel or water.

Days 15-16

Reedy Creek: growing native plants

Our first port of call is Reedy Creek, about 250 kilometres south of Adelaide. I've always wanted to visit Outback Pride, where Mike and Gayle Quarmby pioneered the propagation of indigenous plant species, and have recently handed over the reigns to Kelly and Triscilla of Bushlolly.

Mike and Gayle welcome us with open arms, and we talk about what led them to start Outback Pride. It all began with the loss of their son, Daniel, and the process of healing through others. Listening to their family's story, I'm reminded of how important it is to follow your own path, to find a reason to get up each day, and somehow push on. They talk movingly about life in Alice Springs, where Gayle grew up, as well as in other communities they have forged relationships with over the years, and what they see as the right way forward. Mike takes us through the polytunnels to look at what's growing: saltbush, perilla, muntries, seaspray, lemon aspen. Down the back, we see muntries trees in flower and learn that these are the source of the fresh muntries I've been buying at Biota for years.

Iceplant at
Reedy Creek.

Our visit is brief. Like us, Gayle and Mike are bound for
the bush, with their trailer packed. They are about to head
north into the indigenous communities where they have spent
so much time. I get the feeling that travelling through
remote Australia is something they long for, something they
relish. For me, it's only just begun - but after talking
with them, I'm ready for my next challenge, ready to listen
to my heart. Maybe the land itself, this country, will help
me with that, who knows...

Gayle and Mike Quarmby of Outback Pride,
and Kelly Grady and Triscilla Holborow of Bushlolly.

Dusk is falling as we head west towards the Coorong, a vast sweep of sand that extends for some 130 kilometres to the mouth of the Murray River. I've been there once before, when I went fishing for Coorong mullet with Glenn and Tracey Hill, of Coorong Wild Seafood; however, this time I'm interested in the Goolwa pipis that are harvested by foot on the ocean side of the estuary.

We arrive at Olaf Hanson's house, on Hindmarsh Island. Olaf is a local food hero - he was the chef at Bombora, in Goolwa, for many years - and I'll never forget his generosity that night. He offered us a spot for our swags in his studio, safe from the cold, and greeted us with a warming stew, along with some epic reds, while we talked about food and wine and the region we were in. Unwinding and laughing with newfound friends was very welcome, but we knew we had to be at the wharf before sunrise next day, so we hit the hay early

I love Coorong mullet,
but not seeing Glenn and
Tracy Hill this time ~~unfortunately~~
unfortunately so missing
out on mullet.

Day 17

Goolwa and the Mount Lofty Ranges:
pipis and a last deer hunt

We awake to a panoramic view of the mouth of the Murray
River dotted with paddle steamers - and across the way we
can see Goolwa. I'm really looking forward to spending the
day with Alistair Scott-Young, of the Goolwa Pipi Company.

We jump in the car and roll onto the barge, which only fits
one vehicle. We're loaded up with more than 400 kilos of
gear. It feels bloody sketchy, and all I can think about
is the phone call I'll need to make to Jaguar Land Rover,
explaining that I've accidentally put a new Discovery at the
bottom of the sea. But before we know it, the barge gathers
speed and we're flying across the Coorong. With the sun
coming up and the birds chasing us, it's stunning,
something I'll always remember.

putting the Disco
on a barge to go
across and look
at pipis with
the team from
Goolwa Pipi
Co.

When we drive the car off the barge, the Goolwa Pipis team are
waiting - these seadogs spend long days in icy-cold waters. This is
hard-core. Scattered along the rugged, untamed coastline are small
groups harvesting pipis, and we head down to the water's edge to
learn how it's being done. The guys are barefoot, with big nets in
their hands, and they are shuffling their feet as the waves wash
in and out over the sand. When a wave recedes, it exposes the pipis
and they catch them in the net. The only piece of machinery in this
whole operation is for grading: small pipis go back into the water
and larger ones go on to the truck. Ryan and I are fascinated to
learn that the pipis are harvested this way in all weathers.

In the dunes that back the beach,
Al points out some Aboriginal middens
(off-limits to visitors, as they
are sacred sites) and explains that
the whole coastline here supports a
plethora of edible plants, fish and
birds. He gives us some raw pipis
straight off the beach to try - sashimi
pipis, if you like - and their salinity
and texture are sensational.

We ate these pipis
raw on the beach -
a memory I will
have forever.

The word Coorong is generally accepted to be a corruption of
the local Aboriginal word *kurangh*, meaning 'neck'. Before we
continue our journey north, I want to talk with some of the
indigenous people here, who have timeless connections with
the lower Murray, its lakes and the Coorong. Arthur Walker
and Brian Kropinyeri, of Ngopamuldi Aboriginal Corporation,
tell me stories of these waters, their hunting and gathering
traditions, and what the Coorong means to them - a place
of wind, water and vast skies, sandhills, tussock-fringed
lagoons and waterweeds.

It's almost afternoon by now, and we need to
get on the road before we lose the light. Back
in Goolwa, the priority is food and drink. Adam
gets moody when he hasn't eaten, and Ryan wants
a beer, so we head down to the Goolwa Hotel
for a few frothies - and yep, you guessed it, a
schnitty. A smile lights up Adam's face and later
the local bar girl comes out to offer her phone
number to him. Must be those bald patches, or
maybe the glow in his eyes from the schnitty!

Massive thanks
to Brian and Arthur
for welcoming us to
this special place

Alistair has hooked us up with a mate of his, Tom
Carr, who has a property a short drive north, near
Ashbourne. The plan is to spend the night there and
have another go at a deer hunt - it's probably the
last time we'll see deer on the trip, plus we need
some meat to stock up the fridge before we keep
going north. When we arrive, we settle in for a beer
and a chat with Tom and his partner Laura O'Donnell.
Tom is in a wheelchair from an accident, but he has
a shooting rest and the perfect little set-up on
his own back deck, where he shoots foxes and other
vermin and also does target practice. I could have
stayed here all arvo on the tins with him, and I
know Ryan definitely would have.

Getting setup for
a quick arvo hunt -
we need meat for
our trip

Eventually, we head uphill and pitch camp for the night. I go and set up a hide and wait for the rest of the arvo. Around dusk we see a few little fallow deer with the binos, but they are too far away for a clean and humane shot so I watch and wait. Nothing eventuates, but that's all part of the hunt. Sometimes it's meant to be, and sometimes you come up empty. I guess this teaches us that wild food has no price tag, but is special and when harvested should be respected to the full.

The road
to Whyalla.

Days 18-19

Whyalla and Streaky Bay:
sea salt and razorfish

The next morning, we set off at sunrise for the
five-hour drive northwest to Whyalla. After going
over the Adelaide Hills and down into Adelaide, we
feel some relief at getting out onto the open road
again. Pulling off the freeway into a small town
called Snowtown, I can't resist asking the boys if
they fancy rolling out the swags here for the night.
When we realise Ryan doesn't know about the Snowtown
murders, we Google the story and read it out to him
as we're driving through town, and he's absolutely
wigging out. We're suggesting we stop, telling him
it'll be a barrel of laughs. Obviously, we don't end
up stopping, but Ryan wants his photo taken in front
of the bank - with a tinny in hand, of course.

As we get closer to Whyalla, the landscape becomes more desolate, all red soil and heat beating off the tarmac. We begin to realise that we've way underestimated the distances in South Australia, and we really need to make sure we hit the dirt tracks before the Wet is in full swing - one downpour and the roads become more like river systems. As it is, we're cutting it fine by travelling in the Gulf region during October and November, which is well into the unpredictable weather.

Nature's steaming parcel →

We arrive in Whyalla in the late afternoon, to be greeted by Alex Olsson, of Olsson's Sea Salt, a family-run company that has been in business since 1888. Interestingly, part of the Olsson property was purchased from a former steel refinery - the industry Whyalla is best known for - and we pass through a steel mill to get to the salt flats. Salt-water pumps are used in the process of steel-making, so it all comes together. Alex and I have met before (we use Olsson's salt in all our restaurants) and so we head straight onto the salt flats to make a camp and get cooking. After a long and dusty day on the road, a seafood feast on the coast is just what we all need. We haven't had much time to gather ingredients, but we do have some Goolwa pipis and Leap Farm goat meat in the cooler in the car, and Alex has some whiting and snapper fresh from the Spencer Gulf.

Ryan and I get to work. I go for a wander and find saltbush,
samphire and seablite growing everywhere. We make a little
coastal herb butter to go with the whiting, then wrap the fish
in wet bark from a paperbark tree. Next we dig a pit in the
sand, drop in some hot coals from the fire and add the whiting,
covering it with more sand and leaving it to cook. The snapper
is cooked whole on a bed of samphire, almost steamed, then we
just scrape off the skin and eat the soft white flesh. For the
pipis we make a saltbush and garlic butter - we always carry
garlic! - and simply eat them out of the shell.

Catching up with Alex and sharing a bottle of vino (except for
Ryan the Rhino, who's on the beer again) is perfect. We even
make some samphire-infused cocktails.

Discussing salt pans
with Alex, and how
they're harvested.

The next morning Alex takes us around the plant and shows us how the salt is produced simply by letting the water evaporate from sea water in large ponds the size of football fields. The salt is then harvested by scraping off the layer of salt before it goes through various cleaning and filtering processes. We also take a look at the different forms of salt (blocks, flakes and fine table salt), as well as their salt licks for livestock and agribusiness products.

There is saltbush growing all around the salt pans and ponds. Saltbush has a very deep tap root that draws the water table down with it, preventing the salty water from reaching the surface. In areas where the water table has reached the surface and salinity is a problem, you'll often find that the saltbush has been cleared, and replanting it can help to rehabilitate the land.

Rhino laying a bed
of sea plants to cook
the snapper on.

Inside a razorfish
you'll find a nugget
of scallop-like meat.

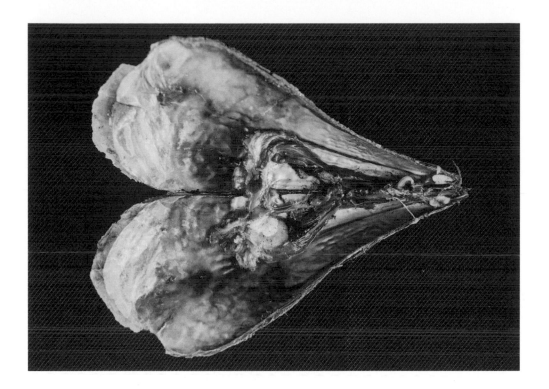

Before we leave the coast and head into the Outback, we go off on a detour to Streaky Bay to see a bloke about some razorfish. A few years back, oyster farmer Reg Brown and his wife, Janine, noticed an influx of razorfish taking over their oyster leases, so they applied for a permit to fish them commercially. These razorfish are an invasive species and, in my opinion, should be on our menus. Yes, they're pricey and hard to catch, but there's no denying they taste great.

Opening a razorfish - delicious eaten raw as well

Reg and Janine have just returned with a catch of
razorfish, and I'm intrigued to try them straight
off the boat. With extremely sharp shells, they
certainly live up to their name, and they have
a large shell for the amount of meat they contain,
but it's beautiful meat, almost like a firm scallop
with a notable fat content. The guts are pretty
significant as well and could potentially be used
to make a fish sauce or garum of some sort.
I already make a garum with mussel guts at the
restaurant, but you could easily do it with
razorfish too.

Streaky Bay
Wharf
↓

By now, the boys look like they need
a frothy. Wayne Hulme, of Joto, who
supplies most of the fish and seafood
we use at Biota, had said that we
couldn't come here without going
to Streaky Bay Seafood for lunch,
so that's what we do, eating some
great whiting out on the pier,
with a few beers.

RYAN KOVAC
Bertha's Meats, Bowral

'I want you to come on the South Australia part of the trip, Rhino,' says James, across the kitchen at Biota. That's how my two-week-long adventure through some of the most memorable and remote parts of Australia came about.

Starting with a flight into Adelaide, I was off to discover what this country has to offer. South Australia was an intense contrast between the hot, saltbush-strewn desert and the cold waters of the great Southern Ocean. Meeting Mike and Gayle Quarmby was a moment I will never forget. Mike talked of scouring Outback Australia for a specific strain of saltbush and only finding it on an island in the middle of a river untouched by livestock and farmers. Seeing Outback Pride's passion for working closely with indigenous people was incredible, and their drive to bring native ingredients to the rest of Australia will be a huge inspiration to me personally, and my cooking, for a long time to come.

Something my family and friends all know about me is that my favourite place to be is that thin line where the ocean meets the land, and so our visit to the Goolwa Pipi Company did not disappoint. Standing knee-deep in the Southern Ocean with powerful waves breaking as far as the eye can see, and with ancient sand dunes rich in indigenous history at my back, was my idea of nirvana.

Jumping in and helping Alistair and his crew harvest pipis from along a 90-kilometre stretch of unbroken sandy beach gave me a real sense of connection to this land's indigenous heritage.

'What do you mean, there's no flights out of Alice Springs? Fuck it. Ryan will just keep heading north.' This is where my journey took an unexpected turn, one that led me across the guts of Australia with James. We travelled through the heart of the Gawler Ranges, a surreal landscape of red dirt, harsh weather-torn scrub and the occasional windmill... someone told me we were going through a sheep farm - but in six hours of driving I never saw one. Arriving in Kingoonya was like taking half a step back into civilisation, in the shape of a tin shed that served cold beer. Good enough. And the friendly faces at Van Rook cattle station marked the end of the adventure, with a few beers and stories being swapped.

Reflecting on my journey, I feel a great sense of pride in the country I call home - from the people I met and shared a cold beer or two with, to the rich abundance of food and ingredients and the ever-changing landscapes. I feel like a very lucky man to have stumbled into such a wonderful opportunity.

Into the
Outback

We're about to drive some of Australia's remotest roads, so we head over to the servo to get everything checked, fill up on fuel and top up our water supplies.

Day 20

Streaky Bay to the Gawler Ranges: snake country and gumbo

Today we're headed for Wirrulla, a small town at the southern end of the Gawler Ranges Road. We're all feeling slightly nervous and tired, and we stop on the way to do a driver change. The car is so full that there's no space for the seat to go back. Adam is crammed in the back with a charging inverter for his camera equipment, a downloading setup for the shots and Ryan (happily, Rhino only needs space for a tinny and some darts).

I'm in the front, and I lose my shit over Ryan trying to adjust the seat and tearing his shirt in the process - not important in the scheme of things, I know, and I go for a walk to calm down. This is where a few weeks of living in such close quarters, missing our loved ones and putting up with each other starts to get to us...

All is soon forgotten when we reach Wirrulla, jump out and see the signs
pointing north. It's hot out, 32°C, and this marks the beginning of the wild
part of the trip - a highlight for all of us, with no set appointments, just
random encounters along the way. When you start seeing road signs saying 'Last
fuel for 400km' and 'Road closed'/'Road open', you know you're off the beaten
track, and this is exactly the medicine I think I need.

At a crossroads →

The stark landscapes of the Gawler Ranges are full of
stunning rock formations, rare native bird species and the
famed yellow-footed rock wallaby. We stop on a dried-out
salt pan to stretch our legs and take it all in - it's
not long before we start to feel very alone out here. The
reality hits us that we're in the middle of the Outback,
with nothing around for several hundred kilometres at least.
This is the best feeling: the anticipation of what lies
ahead as we drive 3,000-plus kilometres of dirt road all
the way to the Gulf of Carpentaria is spiked with adrenalin.
Some of the tracks we're going to be travelling on aren't
even shown on conventional maps...

Night is fast approaching, so we pull over when we reach
a crossroads with a stock route. The good thing is that we
can set up our swags and get a fire going pretty quickly by
now. We're in snake country here - big tiger snakes and king
browns, maybe the odd death adder as well. Not exactly the
most comforting thought, factoring in the issue of sleeping
in a swag. Adam and Ryan go looking for firewood. There's
only some low-lying tea tree scattered around and we can't
help noticing a lot of small holes in the wood where snakes
might be lurking... Not too keen at all on disturbing one
of these bad boys.

We get the fire going and fold down the tailgate of the Disco.
I tell the boys I've got dinner covered tonight. It's so nice to
cook for your friends under the seemingly endless skies of the
Australian Outback: no music, no sound, just nature and the crackle
of the tea tree on the fire - which smells amazing, by the way.
The boys crack open some tinnies. Rhino is already half-cut, it's
been a big afternoon. In the fridge there's the tail-end of an old
salami, along with some whiting and calamari we bought from the fish
shop in Streaky Bay and some beach herbs we picked up in Whyalla,
and it all goes into the pot to make a sort of seafood and sausage
gumbo. We sit around the fire under the stars and enjoy the warmth
and spice of the gumbo before calling it a day.

After about half an hour, just when we've all fallen asleep, we hear another vehicle coming and immediately get up to see what's going on. We wait and wait. In the pitch dark, we can see lights, but they just don't seem to be getting any closer. Finally a car goes past, and the guys yell, 'G'day, mate!', their arms hanging out the windows as they turn onto another road... We drift off to sleep again. The Rhino is snoring like a freight train - it's more accentuated when he's drunk. When it starts to rain in the night, Adam and I zip up inside our swags, but Ryan is passed out and the next morning he wakes up drenched and totally bitten by mozzies.

our campfire setup, dark skies approaching and a wet night for the Rhino →

Day 21

Kokatha land: windmills, wild goats, Coober Pedy and Marla

The next day we push on through the Kokatha indigenous lands, a vast expanse that encompasses some of the harshest and driest terrain on the Australian continent. The road quickly turns from soft red desert sand to slippery shale rock, and we have to slow down. Out here, I can't risk any damage to the car, or to ourselves.

Quick pitstop
ontop of a slight
hill ➤

We finally arrive in central Kokatha, which is just a homestead
really, with a lot of sheep fenced into large pens. I can't help
wondering how long it takes for livestock to be transported
out from here, and I'm thinking the condition they're in when
they reach the abattoir must be pretty ordinary - we're talking
400-500 kilometres from anywhere by now.

We stop and have a look at an old windmill just outside
the settlement. There are a lot of the original Southern
Cross windmills out here. Produced commercially from the
early 1900s, they're all supposed to be individually marked
with a serial number. I look for a plate somewhere on
it, but can't see anything. It still seems to be working
alright and pumping water, though, so we have a drink of
the metallic-tasting water and a bit of a refreshing wash
as well. In these parts, you have to take the opportunity
to wash when you can!

Driving on, we come across a huge mob of wild
goats, I'm talking 200-plus goats. They just
meander across the track in front of us. Some
of the bucks are massive and as we're running
low on food we're tempted to shoot one for
meat - but we're in a national park and can't
use firearms without permission.

Wild goats in
the Gawler Ranges

We eventually roll into Kingoonya, the first town we've seen
in days of driving, and it's pretty confronting: the houses,
really more like sheds, are just standing. There's an eerie
atmosphere, as if the place has been forgotten. Once a vital
link in the Trans-Australian railway, for many years the
township relied on the Tea and Sugar train for its weekly
supplies, but now trains no longer stop here and it has an
abandoned air about it.

We were planning to stay the night here,
but by the looks of it, I'd sooner sleep
out under the stars again somewhere down
the track. We pull up in front of the only
public house - little more than a tin shed
with XXXX written all over it - and peel
ourselves off the car seats.

A bloke in a pair of stubbies and a bluey yells out, 'Christ,
she looks too low to be driving around these parts, mate!'
I explain that the chassis can be raised up and down, depending
on the terrain, and we'd lowered it so we could easily get out.
Well, he's infatuated with it. Up here, it seems everybody drives
a Land Cruiser, but the Discovery is holding up well, and so
far all I've needed to do to keep this wagon on the road is
pump up the tyres after a beach expedition. Touch wood!

The idiot
box ↘

After a few beers and a chat with some blokes
who are also just passing through, we decide to
move on. We're headed towards Coober Pedy, about
400 kilometres away via Tarcoola. As we drive over
the sand-covered rail lines, the road widens and
quickly becomes full of sand ruts and washouts –
this goes on for 250 kilometres until we hit the
Stuart Highway, a long-awaited stretch of bitumen.

No sooner are we on the highway than we see a city runabout pulled off
to the side of the road with three young backpackers alongside it, looking
extremely lost and insecure. We decide to take a look. Now I don't admit
to knowing much about engines, but I do know when one is fucked, and this
little car is well fucked. That's what happens when you drive through
central Australia with no oil. These kids had bought a car from a bloke
in Coober Pedy, who obviously buys shitty little cars and then flogs them
off to unknowing backpackers - this one had probably done three laps around
Australia already.

Kingoonya
rental cars

We decide to leave two of them with the broken-down car and take the other
guy, a young German, into Coober Pedy to sort the issue with the bloke he
bought the car from. He jumps in the back of the Disco, squeezing in between
Adam and a Remington 243. I'm sure *Wolf Creek* is crossing his mind by this
stage, so we cover up the rifle with Ryan's ripped shirt from earlier.
When we drop him off at the bloke's house, we feel like we should stick
around to see what happens — but time is slipping away from us and we have
to keep driving north.

We go off to explore Coober Pedy. We aren't there
long until we all start to notice the same vibe
happening - and we're not talking opals, but
a bucket-load of crap 'Straya souvenirs. Every
second shop is a souvenir shop, and the place feels
strangely unreal, like walking through a Sim City...
I guess that's to be expected when you're on the
road more frequently travelled (same goes in life,
really), but I can't wait to pull off the tarmac and
hit some dirt and diversity again, to connect with
the natural world. Get me the fuck out of here!

We leave town on the Stuart Highway, happy to see the back of the big Hollywood-hillside-knockoff 'Coober Pedy' sign. After a few more hours behind the wheel, we reach a small town called Marla, still in South Australia. We feel like we've been driving for a bloody long time, and thought we would surely be in the Northern Territory by now; not the case.

not my favorite place
happy to ~~or~~ see the
↙ back of it

The town takes its name from the Marla bore, which is itself
a corruption of the Aboriginal *marlu*, meaning 'kangaroo'. Marla
is not very big, with a population of about 100, but it's got
a massive servo and an overnight campground, with hot showers -
that's right, hot showers! Unanimously we decide to wheel in,
grab a roast dinner from the servo (pretty crook, actually)
and then a shower to wash away the sins of our dinner choice.

Day 22

The Stuart Highway to Alice and onto the
Sandover Highway: desperate for diesel

Next morning, we get an early start and press on
towards Alice Springs, a monotonous seven-hour drive
away on the Stuart Highway.

On this trip I told myself I didn't want to go
to any of the big tourist attractions, especially
if I've been there before. I didn't want to visit
sights just to get the obligatory shot, so if
you don't see a photo of Uluru (Ayers Rock) in
here it's because I've been there already, and
because you can Google it. I was after the kind
of images and experiences you can't Google - the
real Australia and the spontaneity of meeting
people in the most unlikely places.

One of the local
station owners near
Marla. Great talks
over a cold beer about
their station, their
land and its people.

I lost

We stop around the halfway point at a roadhouse
in the middle of nowhere. It's pissing down, which
has me worried for the next 2,500 kilometres we
are yet to travel. Remote roadhouses like this
one usually have facilities like a bar (a must
out here), a campground and a shop that sells the
basic necessities and fuel. It's about 11am, and
we sit down in the bar area, which is completely
empty apart from three indigenous guys who own and
operate a huge cattle station nearby, as well as
this roadhouse. They are kicking back until the rain
eases, and we enjoy having a chat with them about
their lands, and what the future holds for the land
they farm. Also, one of them is a shark on the pool
table: I have a few rounds with him and then call it
once I've been beaten more than a handful of times.

When we jump back in the car and head north to Alice Springs, it's still pissing down... If the Wet settles in, we won't be able to keep going. When it's been dry for so long and the land is arid, the water just sits on top of the soil and doesn't seep in, meaning nasty, nasty road conditions, washouts and real danger.

We don't stay in Alice for long. Really, the only reason we're
here is the airport: we're dropping off Adam, who needs to check
in with his young family after being on the road for a few weeks,
and picking up Tim West, the sous-chef from Biota. While the boys
get a late lunch, I do some ringing around: I'm trying to get a
gauge of the Sandover Highway, some 750 kilometres of dirt track
that heads northeast towards Queensland. It isn't used much, and
for most of the way you are crossing the traditional lands of the
Alyawarra people. It has unknown hazards - sandhills, corrugations
and black-soil plains that are an impassable quagmire after rain.
During the Wet, Alpurrurulam (Lake Nash), near the border with
Queensland, becomes completely inaccessible, so we are going to
have to check on the weather conditions at Arlparra, an indigenous
community about a third of the way along.

These roads require constant focus — they are tiring and relentless →

For months I've been researching this road and
getting no real answers. I call the local police
stations, but they don't know a lot either -
all they say is that it's remote. We're carrying
plenty of water and spare fuel (apparently
the longest run between fuel stops is around
320 kilometres), and our car is equipped with
Hema off-road maps and access to real-time
satellite weather information...

Soon we find ourselves at the start of the Sandover Highway, about 200 kilometres from Alice. It's unnerving to think that we're about to drive on one of the most remote roads in Australia, with no network coverage and no idea of the road conditions. The sky is blue, with low grey clouds scudding across it, and the track is sticky from some earlier rain; not too bad, though. But the sign says it all: 'Dangerous road conditions ahead'.

Tim, Ryan and I step outside the car to talk about whether or not we do this, or just go on the Plenty Highway instead. I'm in two minds. I'm doing this trip because I want to see this country for all its challenges. I want it to challenge me to my fullest, and I also hope it opens the hearts and minds of my fellow travellers. Just as we are trying to decide, a white Falcon comes charging down the track: it's missing its front bumper and the back bumper is hanging off. I walk out into the middle of the road to flag down the people in the car so I can ask them what the conditions are like. They stop, reluctantly (I wouldn't stop for me, either), and I see they're an Aboriginal family. I ask about the road, and in a very deep, almost shy voice, the driver says, 'Good', and then drives off. In this moment, I'm thinking to myself that maybe I really don't belong here. The guy spoke in broken English, which is of course fine - it's us who are the strangers here, passing through Aboriginal lands - but, for a fleeting moment, standing there in the heart of this country, for the first time in my life, I feel like I don't belong here, like I'm a guest, and it's a good, honest feeling in a way.

Excited at the news that the road is passable, we all jump in the Disco. The boys are saying, 'We're doing this', 'We gunna do this'. We want to calculate the fuel usage, and the car starts to work out what fuel we will need as it adjusts to the road conditions. We're sitting on 70 kilometres per hour and the road is okay, a little sandy with some pretty soft edges, but I pick a line on the top of the road and stick to it. We notice that we're not seeing any kangaroos or wildlife, the odd eagle but not a great deal of emu or anything else; it's just such a different landscape. It is vast, and the soil is the reddest soil I've seen. There's spinifex everywhere and it's flat.

We're only about 30 kilometres in when the road starts to get nasty, with sand ruts and washouts that I'm struggling to see in the slanting afternoon light. It's about 4pm and the day is disappearing. I drop the speed but that doesn't help, so I set the Disco to 'sand' mode and increase my speed to 80 kilometres per hour. It digs in like it's on rails - what a beast, it's just eating up these conditions.

Red dirt gets into everything →

Rhino found
a spare shoe
here ↓

We stop for a roadside dinner about two
hours from Arlparra, and I go for a
little wander to see if there's anything
other than spinifex. I don't see any
trees or signs of food, and we don't want
to camp just anywhere as a lot of the
land here is native title, which means we
can drive through on the road, but can't
go off-road without written consent from
the community. Dinner consists of cooler
leftovers - nothing to hunt and no water
to fish in means slim pickings, but we're
all keen to eat quickly and push on, as
we have a long road ahead of us.

We finally reach Arlparra, where we need to fill up on fuel. We have
around 400 kilometres' worth of fuel left in the tank and about 40 litres
in cans on the roof, so we might make it, but there's no buffer. Our fuel
calculations are based on the assumption that we make it out the other side
and don't need to turn around, so I want to fill up as a precaution.

When we pull in, it's like a ghost town - the small
petrol station is empty and the bowsers have locks on
them. Now, for those who've never been to an indigenous
community in the Outback, it's an eye-opener. The modest
houses are more like tin sheds and are built directly
on the ground, there are no gardens or grass and it's
bloody dry out here. However, it's a community, and
there's a school (I actually contacted them to see if
we could stop and do some cooking with the kids, but
they were on holidays when we were passing through,
which is a shame).

I decide to go for a walk to find somebody, but I can't find a soul - apart from two guys hanging out of a car doing burn-outs about half a kilometre away, and I decide to leave them to it. By now it's getting late and dark. As I'm wandering around, the setting sun is creating shadows on the walls of the buildings and around the baseball court and I notice they're painted with beautiful indigenous artwork. It takes a little while to tune in to it, but there is a lot of beauty in this place. Later I find out that Arlparra is in the Utopia region, which is world-famous for its Aboriginal art.

We push on towards Alpurrurulam, about another 600 kilometres, give or take... By now, it's dark and we are officially worried about our fuel situation. On the maps I notice that there is a cattle station nearby. Now most of the stations round here are not too keen on people entering their property - what with it being so vast and so remote, there is a lot of livestock theft, as well as burglary. And normally, there is nothing worse than driving off the main road into an unknown place, let alone somebody else's home, without any warning or prior arrangement, but we are desperate.

Local artwork in a covered shelter in the community of Arlparra.

We drive through the big entrance into Ammaroo Station and
up to the work shed, where a young bloke in a skid steer
is packing up for the day. He doesn't notice us and walks
on inside. As he's walking across the perfect green lawns,
surrounded by bull dust, I call out, 'G'day, mate!' He turns
around and says, 'G'day'. I stay where I am, so as not to
intrude, and explain that we're looking to buy some diesel.
He yells out, 'Mum, somebody's here...' A lady who looks
like she has talked to every bloody bull in every paddock
comes out. I mean, these guys look like they work so fucking
hard each day, and here I am at their family home, pestering
them at knock-off time for fuel. I feel pretty bloody bad.
I can tell she's wary of us, not unreasonably, but she
says, 'How can I help?' I ask if I can buy some fuel. Anna,
her name is Anna, says, 'Sure, how much worth?' I scramble
around the car for money, and we find $40 between us... that
should give us enough to get to Gregory Downs at least.

There's something about travelling through the bush and
meeting people like Anna. I don't know Anna and her family,
but what I can tell you is that genuine, good-hearted and
kind people are everywhere around us. Anna, you and your
family saved our asses that day - and if you ever read this
book, thank you.

By now we're all wide awake and decide to just keep on
driving... We're not sure of the road ahead and it's dark,
but the night sky is the brightest I've ever seen. Tim is
having a nap in the back and Rhino and I are up the front.
The track is alive at night with tiger snakes that span the
entire width of the road, and the headlights cut through
insects the size of small budgies. I'm on a mission: this
road requires complete focus, even more so at night.

I take a look at the maps, comparing routes and tracks. The
decision to be made is whether to stay on the Sandover all the
way to Alpurrurulam and run the risk of road closures due to poor
conditions, or turn off about 20 kilometres sooner, onto a track
that will take us up to join the Barkly Highway and then into
Camooweal, across the border in Queensland. The issue is that the
other track is not mapped - it's a road through Austral Downs,
a cattle station that occupies an area of about 469,000 hectares.
I decide to take the turn off: it's a narrow road running along
a fenceline and it leads to a closed gate that says 'Private
Property', but we open it and carry on driving. Most of these big
stations have through-roads you can drive on, as long as you don't
venture off the road.

It's about midnight now, and I'm starting to fade...
Mind you, by taking this route we have essentially gone
from South Australia to central Queensland, via the Northern
Territory, in one massive hit. To give you an idea of the
distances involved and the time it takes to cover them,
we've just spent four and a half hours driving across just
this one property. At one point I veer off the track to
miss a bull standing in the middle of the road - this isn't
uncommon in these parts, and it's pretty dangerous to be
driving at night, but we can't stop on Austral Downs, let
alone make a camp, so we just have to keep going until we
get to Camooweal.

We finally pull off the dirt onto the bitumen of the mighty
Barkly Highway and drive into Camooweal, wrecked. We roll
out the swags and sleep comes quickly.

TIM WEST
Biota, Bowral

Sitting at Sydney airport, I can feel myself getting more and more nervous, not because of the flight but because of all the unknowns. I have no return flight booked, no idea what to expect, and no idea what I'm doing, where I'm going, what I'll see or eat, or who I'll meet. All I have is a bag full of undies, a camera and a fishing lure that I had to fight airport security to keep - you're welcome, Ryan!

James Viles, my boss and mentor, is going to meet me in Alice Springs. All I know is that we're driving to be inspired: by the people, the produce, the land, the journey, the stories and the friendships. Essentially, this is an R and D trip for the next phase of Biota and I keep telling myself that I just need to take notes, take photos, listen and be open...

We're soon in the middle of nowhere, and I can't believe we just drove one of the most challenging roads in Australia at night. James was determined to get through it, no way was he stopping short of it - his determination is second to none. Next day we're still driving off-road when we get a flat tyre. It's over 40°C and we only have one spare, but I guess it wouldn't be a Biota trip without some suspense! After nursing the car for three hours, it's a massive relief to roll into a service station, where I eat the most amazing mango of my life so far. Warmed by the sun all day, it tastes incredible.

On the drive to Gulf Country I'm riding shotgun, quite literally. A rifle barrel is hard up against my thigh and, I'm not going to lie, it's making me a little bit nervous. I've never really been comfortable around guns, and I'm not sure how I'll get on if James asks me if I want to have a go at shooting. Note to self: if you see a boar, hit it! Or, as James says, 'Do anything under the sun to kill it - it's a bloody pest, Timmo, don't feel guilty.'

When we reach Van Rook Station, it strikes me as an unbelievable place, like something out of an old American movie set in the Deep South, around Mississippi or New Orleans; it just has that vibe about it. Barramundi fishing as the sun sets is a pretty special way to end the day.

Gulf
Country

————————— —————— —————————— ———

After the Sandover, we feel like the hardest road of the
trip is behind us. We've clocked up nearly 17 hours without
stopping except for fuel, staying above 80 kilometres per
hour to avoid sinking into the sand. We feel drunk on all
the driving; our eyes are stinging from the strain of
focusing in the darkness.

Day 23

Camooweal to Karumba:
greasy beginnings, a purple pub
and a crumbed steak

In the morning, we arise from our comas, feeling like
we've been hit by a road train. I need grease, a big
greasy brekky, and a shower. Between the three of us,
the car is starting to smell like warm taco meat. We
shower in the caravan park - it's another coin-operated
number... and I don't have enough coins to wash off the
ordeal of driving through such unforgiving terrain.

> Anyway, all showered and fresh, we
> head into the big smoke (population
> 184) in search of breakfast. The
> local servo/truck stop seems to be
> the way to go. A cheeky bogan dust
> and an egg and bacon roll serves
> its purpose as we look at the maps.
> So far we've travelled just on 8,560
> kilometres, and the car is screaming
> out for AdBlue. Luckily, this truck
> stop sells it, so we do a top-up.

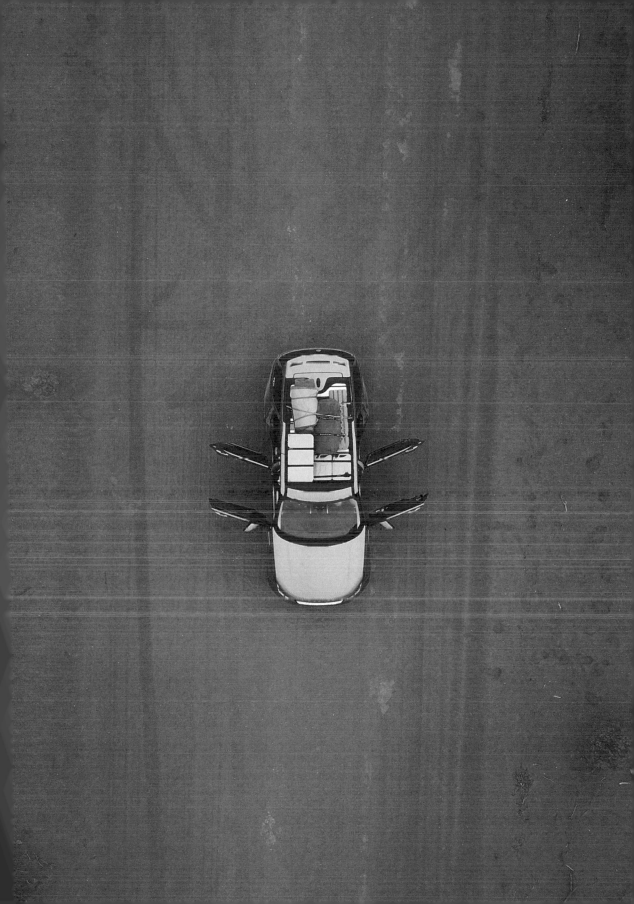

The next stretch of road is about 400 kilometres long
and goes from Camooweal to Normanton, via the Gregory
Downs Camooweal Road and the Wills Developmental Road,
and we're just guessing at the ten hours of driving we
think it will take to reach the Gulf of Carpentaria.

On the way to the turn-off we come across an injured wedge-tailed
eagle - it looks like it has been hit by a car or truck, and sadly
it is too late for us to save it. Such majestic, beautiful creatures
like this are amazing to see close up; its wingspan must be at least
1.6 metres. I pull a feather from its outer wing and keep it for
luck, then leave its body to the side of the road for the earth to
consume over time.

We reach the Gregory Downs Camooweal Road, take one
look and think to ourselves, *What are we doing?* Let
me tell you, this road is not a road: it is sharp
rocks the size of my fist, deep washouts from previous
flooding and no fuel or stops. But it's either this
or the long way round, which would mean two more days
until we reach the Gulf. We've been trying to head due
north the whole trip, trying to beat the Wet season,
so taking the easy road isn't really an option. It's
already the end of October, and we need to get there
before the rain comes and makes the roads impassable...

This is Barkly Tableland country: you can see where the water has
been rushing through, forming gullies and deltas, wiping out trees
and fences as it goes; the road is sketchy and honestly not pleasant.
By the roadside, we see some trees with yellow berries. Called soap
trees, these were used in a traditional fishing method: Aborigines would
crush the berries and leaves to a pulp and then release it into a pool
full of fish. A soap-like film would coat the surface of the water and,
starved of oxygen, the stunned fish would rise to the surface, where they
could be easily caught. On the same road I notice a lot of flowering gum
and we pick some to make tea - a nice and refreshing chilled bush tea.

Some flowering gum to make → Bush tea with

Not long afterwards, this shitty road rips one of our tyres.
And not a small hole either - it's completely torn apart,
leaving us with only one spare tyre to get to Normanton.
So we take it easy for the rest of the drive, finally
reaching Gregory and the very welcome sight of the Gregory
Downs Hotel. Now, this is a pub. Originally built to serve
passengers on the coach run from Burketown, the hotel is
right next to the perennially-flowing Gregory River, a river
perfect for three men to have a wash. We sit at the bar,
drinking the coldest XXXX we've had in days (it's more than
30°C outside) and hanging around for a couple of hours.
Apparently the place has a population of about 40, but we
didn't see any of them, apart from the bar girls!

After driving from Gregory via some pretty boring bitumen roads, we arrive in the small town of Normanton. I've actually been to Normanton on a few occasions - with its tiny little airport, it acts as a stopping-off point to get to Karumba and Van Rook Station. It's one of those gateway towns, and it feels like it too.

We drive past a replica of Krys, supposedly the largest saltwater crocodile ever captured, which was recorded as 28 feet 4 inches (8.63 metres) long. The story goes that the croc was shot by Krystina Pawloski in July 1957 in the Norman River, and sure enough, it's a huge beast. Its head is bigger than the bonnet of the Discovery, and I'm beginning to think there might be an element of never letting the truth get in the way of a good story about it all. We head over to the local garage to sort out a new tyre, then we crack a beer at the town's famous Purple Pub before driving on to Karumba.

Normanton airport in all its glory

Green tree
ants →

Karumba's access to the waters of the Gulf of
Carpentaria has made it a prominent fishing port,
and I sometimes use Gulf prawns, mud crab and
barramundi from here at Biota. There are massive
boats everywhere, often bigger than the houses
they're parked in front of. I spent some time here
before planning this trip, scouring the land and
finding the many ingredients that can be eaten,
both plant and animal-based: as well as fishing
for barra, we'll be scouring the place for green
tree ants and wild coastal greens.

By this stage we haven't slept in a real bed since Flinders Island,
so we all agree to live it up a little in Karumba, treating ourselves
to a nice hot dinner and an apartment at the beachfront End of the
Road Motel. We check into our rooms and jump into the retro motel
pool, feeling like Hollywood porn stars as we loll around poolside
on colourful Acapulco-style chairs. The climax to the evening is
polishing off a good old-fashioned country steak (crumbed, of course -
that way you can't tell how old it is), getting on the tins at the
Karumba pub and watching the sun go down... which quickly turns into
watching the insides of our eyelids about ten minutes later.

The Gulf of Carpentaria and Cape York:
sleeping under the stars and eating
from the land

Adam is back on board today, and we're travelling 150 kilometres
north of Karumba (about two hours on dirt roads) to the Gulf Coast
Agricultural Co. Combining four stations (Inkerman, Dorunda, Van Rook
and Stirling Lotus Vale), this extensive property covers more than
a million hectares of the Cape York Peninsula and 90 kilometres of
coastline along the Gulf of Carpentaria, and runs more than 100,000
pure Brahman cattle. This is where I've arranged to meet up and
hang out with like minded chefs Mark LaBrooy, Lennox Hastie, Paul
Carmichael, Beau Clugston and David Moyle, all flying in tomorrow. The
general idea is to sleep under the stars for a few days, and to eat
only what we gather in terms of wild ingredients each day.

Magpie Geese

The next day we greet the guys on Van Rook's dusty airstrip and walk over to the homestead for a cold beer and to get a plan together. We have a campsite in mind; however, there are so many wonders here that we're spoilt for choice. The amazing river systems come alive after the big Wet, and it's on its way. There's already been some rain, and the wetlands are thronging with birdlife, including magpie geese. An important Aboriginal food source, these waterbirds lay eggs in large nests among the lilypads, and the young are raised by both the male and the female. We agree to make our way to Stirling Lotus Vale, about forty-five minutes away by car, where we'll set up camp on the banks of the Gilbert River.

On the way we stop to watch some mustering of a large
mob of Brahman cattle, about 2,000 head, done with
horses and a R22 chopper - it's pretty exhilarating to
watch these cattle on the move like this. We get to the
riverbank and start clearing a space for our swags,
tents and cooking area. It's nice to watch everybody
doing what they do best: Lennox gets straight onto the
building of a makeshift grill and cooking set-up, Marky
sets about organising anything adventure-driven, Dave
gets onto collecting firewood with Beau, and Paul looks
for a fishing rod to start catching some fish for
dinner, likely to be a barra in these parts.

I think it's going to be interesting to see
how six chefs get on in a relatively hostile
environment with no food apart from a few
bare essentials, no proper beds, no mobile
reception and no real bearing on where we
are. The first night we eat some barra that
Paul has caught, simply cooked over the
coals, and then hit the sack, as everybody
is pretty tired.

Our catch.

The next morning, a chopper takes three of us to some of the remoter areas for more fishing. The remainder of us split up and take two Land Cruisers hunting - we're on the lookout for wild ducks, magpie geese and wild suckling pigs. We're also going to forage for native plants and check out the fish species in various waterholes.

~~placing~~
placing mud
crabs

All six of us share a common interest in nature: as cooks we are inspired by what it has to offer, but we let it influence our cooking, and us as humans, in different ways. I personally get a lot out of seeing where the ingredients I use come from, and their natural habitat. Being in such a remote environment also makes me question my presence in the natural world, and the longer I am here, the more I seem to develop heightened senses and a deeper respect for what's around me. I hope that the guys on the trip will find some small connection to this land and what it's always provided.

After a second night of listening to Lennox and Paul
snoring - it's almost rhythmic, reminiscent of wild
boars mating. We have a cup of joe around the fire and
discuss the day's proceedings: today we are going to do
a killer. On cattle stations like this one, all across
Australia, it's always been a tradition to do a killer
and then the whole beast is shared with all the staff,
from the ringers to the managers.

Breaking down a beast
- a vital part of
station life ➞

Next morning, we're keen to resume our search for
wild game and plants, so we split up again (some
in the chopper and some in the Cruisers), this time
for a full day out. On our wishlist are a young pig,
whistling ducks and of course barra, as well as mud
crabs and giant river prawns - all in abundance up
here. I'm on the pig detail with Lennox and Mark,
Paul is on barra or saratoga, and Dave and Beau are
on wild birds. We have pots in for muddies and giant
river prawns, baited with bits of wallaby, which is
considered a pest up here.

Lotus, comes up
in the wet

Perfect little spot
for mud crabs.

Inkerman
coastline.

Lennox and I are in the chopper, along with our friend Riley Aitken, when we spot a mob of pigs: there's a large boar, a couple of sows and some young suckers running across the plain. Only thing is, we have no guns with us, they're back at camp, as we were just refuelling before we went out hunting. The pilot's voice comes through the headphones, saying, 'I'll place you guys on the ground in that scrub over there, you hide and lay low and then I'll push them your way with the chopper.' So we jump out with no rifle, and Riley hands us a pocket knife. There would have to be at least fifteen pigs in this mob, and they are wild pigs, razorbacks...

Heaps of emus about this time of year too.

I don't think I've ever been so afraid in my life; it all happened so quickly. The mob of pigs started running at full speed towards us, the boar screaming and scary, and the little suckers darting off each and every way into the scrub. Lennox and I dive on one each, but they get away, they are so strong and noisy - as the pig slips through my hands it feels like a wire brush. We look over and Riley has one in his arms, pinned to the ground. I gently reach under and take its life with the pocket knife. We lift it into the chopper, our hearts beating furiously, full of adrenalin and scared all at the same time. When the other guys finally get back, Mark has footage of a barra he caught that was 1.24 metres long, a breeder that he put back, and a cooler full of good-sized edible barra.

Beau and Dave come back with loads of whistling
ducks and a couple of magpie geese. We spend
the afternoon cleaning the birds and the fish,
checking the crabpots for muddies and planning
our last evening under the stars. Dinner is a
feast of wild food shared around the fire on the
banks of the Gilbert River. I bring a goanna to
try: yesterday we dug a pit in the smouldering
coals and placed the whole goanna in there, skin
and all, then left it to cook overnight. Lennox
pulls the goanna from the coals and we all taste
it - the meat is dry and white, like pork or
chicken breast meat, but very stringy.

Breaking down
whistling ducks
for dinner.

Emu jerky.

Mud crab pulled
from the waters
up here.

Next up is a mudcrab congee cooked over the
campfire, then we have some whole slow roasted
whistling ducks. With half the ducks we pound the
breast meat into schnitties and pan-fry them. We
also have magpie goose breasts, the beef ribs from
the killer and grilled roti, courtesy of Paul.
Not a lot of greens, admittedly - the season for
samphire and other wild coastal plants in these
parts has been and gone. There are green ants,
but it would take an awful lot of these to make a
satisfying meal. I also make some campfire jaffles
with oxtail inside. There is nothing better than
spending a night cooking and eating in the wild,
and it gives the whole experience perspective to
share in the hunting and gathering. A bond is
formed with each other and with nature.

↑
*oxtail jaffles
for the crew*

Freshwater
crocodile
on the move

We wake in the morning and pack up camp, which takes
a few trips. Back at the homestead we reflect on the
past four days, how lucky we all are to have had an
opportunity to spend time in this unique environment,
and to meet the hard-working people who farm the land.
We've all been inspired by their generosity, love of
food and sense of adventure.

Paul, me and Beau.

All too soon, the other guys fly out, and it feels like watching your best mates leave your birthday party when you were a little boy... We later depart by road to Cairns, a brief and easy drive over the Atherton Ranges, where we leave this journey.

NORMANTON

PAUL CARMICHAEL
Momofuku Seiobo, Sydney

I came to Australia in 2015 not knowing anything about the country aside from a few random facts related to sports or Steve Irwin – and, truthfully, it might well be the best thing I have ever done. It reignited my curiosity and gave me the opportunity to explore like a child. I finally felt like myself again. There is so much to see, so much to do, so much to learn, so much to eat! For the last four years, I have been trying so damn hard to explore this entire country, and I still haven't even scratched the surface.

I won't go all cheffy on you and talk about how great the produce is in the Land Down Under – there are plenty of great Australian cookbooks that will tell you that already. I won't even talk about how beautiful and biodiverse it is – plenty of people smarter than me will write about that as well. Yes, I do love all of that and find those topics interesting, but not this time. What I want to talk about here is people and community, two things that are very important to me.

I find connecting with people in a way that is meaningful to me to be very difficult these days. Too many people are so concerned with the number of 'likes' they get, and what others are doing, that they lose sight of the people right in front of them. I must take some responsibility as well, because I don't really participate in the main ways people connect these days either: man on an island, I guess, literally and figuratively.

Luckily, despite that, I have formed strong bonds with some amazing human beings and have found a real community here. The hospitality industry, in particular, has welcomed me with open arms, and I would need a few pages to mention the countless names and wonderful stories. I still get a little emotional whenever I try to take stock of it all.

When I came to Australia I was not, personally, in the best of places and, without a doubt, the openness I have experienced has helped me to turn that around. I have been accepted in a way I could never have imagined, and for that I will be forever grateful. There is a wholeness to my little community, a gentleness and a seemingly instinctive warmth and honesty – it reminds me of where I grew up, and it just feels good.

BEAU CLUGSTON
Iluka, Copenhagen

Like most people when it comes to their homeland, I love where I come from: the people, the weather, the ocean and the landscape.

227

But it wasn't until my first research trip with noma, back in 2016, that I really felt a true connection to Australia. We travelled the whole country - from Flinders Island and Margaret River to the Top End and everywhere between. But one particular experience in Arnhemland had a profound effect on me. We met with the elders and went foraging on their country. We made spears to catch mud crabs, collected firewood for cooking, gathered cockles and clams at low tide, and hunted kangaroo and water buffalo. After searching for the perfect rock (smooth, but sharp) we sat around the recently lit fire and used the rock to scrape the hairs off the tail of the roo. We then wrapped it in paperbark we'd collected and buried it in the sand about a foot from the fire to confit in its own juices. We put the seafood on the warm coals and waited until it whistled - it was then we knew it was ready.

Being a cook and witnessing a large group of people sitting in complete silence around a fire, giving a blessing to the land for their food, and seeing the joy and happiness in their eyes from eating it, really shook my world. As did tasting produce so fresh that it was embarrassing to think what my own standard of fresh was...

Fast forward a year or two and James Viles invites me on an excursion with a bunch of amazing chefs to the Top End of Australia to eat and live off the land. Although by Australian standards it's relatively close to where I grew up, the food, the land, the people and the vegetation are so different. Once again I feel like an apprentice in my own country. We camp under the stars, fish for barramundi, hunt wild pigs and birds and then sit around a campfire and have the meal of our lives.

The similarity lies in the freshness of the ingredients. I now base my whole restaurant (my life gamble) on these lessons I was taught in the bush. Australia will always be my inspiration, and I'm very lucky to still call it home.

LENNOX HASTIE
Firedoor, Sydney

For me, Australia is a land of boundless potential. Its wide horizons embrace a vast and vivid landscape bursting with life and colour, from the vibrant beaches of its coastline to the richness of its red centre and the vast floodplains of the far north. You could travel far and wide and still not discover all the secret places in Australia.

Our food culture is a profound melting pot of the many ethnic communities that have migrated to Australia and the diversity of produce found here - and it is these stories of Australia's people and ingredients that provide me with a constant source of inspiration.

MARK LABROOY
Three Blue Ducks, Sydney

In recent years I have been lucky
enough to be able to explore some
of our amazing country, and what I
have realised is that we live in one
of the most extraordinary places
on earth: we have such diverse
landscapes, harbouring a treasure
trove of edible and medicinal flora
and fauna.

In the past, my focus was mostly on
the ocean and what lies beneath. As
an avid spearfisherman, it's only
natural that I listen to what the
ocean is communicating to us... When
do the snapper arrive? When do the
cuttlefish or bluefin tuna run? What
can these events tell us about the
changing seasons, the currents in the
water, its temperature and clarity?
The ocean has been good to me, it
has fed me and my family ever since
I first picked up a speargun over
twenty years ago.

James was always more focused on the
land. His love for the bush, hunting
and gathering is infectious, and
he has shown me parts of Australia
I didn't know existed. We have
shared many hunts together, chasing
the elusive deer of NSW with some
success. We have cooked over open
fires and then eaten the organ meat
from the day's hunt, shared stories

and supported each other regarding
our restaurants.

Our stay in the Gulf of Carpenteria
on this latest trip opened my eyes to
the size and scope of our incredible
country - it reminded me of the
freedom we have to explore and enjoy
the outdoors, and the connection I
feel to the land.

Being a hunter and spending so much
time in places off the beaten track
has made me an even stronger advocate
of protecting what we have left. It
has also made me fearful for our land
and waterways, and made me realise
the urgency of reconnecting with our
environment and the way it is managed
if we are to secure its future.

Developing a deep connection to the
land and oceans is not a hobby or
a sport, it's a way of life. I feel
so nourished by the time I spend
outdoors and under the sea that it
helps me to be a better person,
and I believe that this need for
engagement with nature is deeply
embedded in our DNA.

Afterword

Listen

Home now - and with many memories of a trip that was full
of expectations and demands I put on myself: timelines,
dates of where we needed to be when, the imperative of
constantly heading north from Hobart...

It all started in Bowral. I drove to Port Melbourne in a
day, went on the big red boat to Tasmania, hopped across to
Flinders and back, then on to South Australia, the Northern
Territory and Far North Queensland - about 13,000 kilometres
all up. I did this at a stressful time in my life. I had
just wrapped up a two-year contract in Indonesia that had
involved extensive travel every month, we were doing some
renovations at home (we all know how stressful that can
be), and on top of that I was losing key staff that I had
invested time and money into (and we all know what that's
like, no matter what industry we are in). I knew I would
miss both my family and my work, but still I felt this was
something I had to do.

I needed to clear my head. After eight years at Biota, I
was tired and in a rut. And we all know what that's like
too: we're all tired and we all have things we wrestle with
on a daily basis. The thing is to realise what's important
before it's too late. I turned 40 this year, and having
driven myself hard my whole life, I'm no longer thinking
about achievements. Like so many of us in the restaurant
business, I feel I've missed out on spending time with
my wife, my children and my friends; I've missed out on
mother nature; and I've missed out on myself.

But I haven't missed out altogether. I chose the bed I'm
lying in. I love food, I love produce and I love cooking -
and, for a kid who grew up not loving school, they have
opened up a world of opportunity I could never have dreamt
of. It gives me happiness to see young people excelling
in our industry and loving it for all it has to offer.
If any of you are reading this, please do what you love,
but try to keep things in balance and remember to look
after yourself too.

When I got back from writing this journal at the end of October 2018, I was feeling dazed and confused. In a way, it felt like I needed to fit into society again, it felt like a forced reboot - something I wasn't prepared for at all. I came back and went straight to work. We had a family holiday booked at the end of November, so I went at it full-tilt again. Only this time my body wasn't having a bar of it. I was forgetting things and then, in the first week of November, I had a seizure out at Barn, our little project near Biota, on the morning of an event we were doing... It had all added up, it was a big one and I felt like shit.

There and then, I decided I was too old not to start looking after myself. I took a lot of rest (in fact, this book is delayed as a result) and decided I would try to take better care of myself - hopefully, in turn, giving my family and colleagues a better version of me to be around.

The journey I had made through Australia was not just about nature, people and food, it was also about my own personal journey. Now I only want to do things that inspire me, because if I'm inspired, I have a chance of inspiring others too. I'm not wasting time on the chase anymore. I'm after one thing, and that's reality. The reality is that we're all here once, so do once for real.

If I got anything out of this trip, it's that it's vital to challenge yourself and remove yourself from your safe place - but, when the time comes, you need to listen, and listen fucking carefully. Push yourself to your limits, but realise what your limits are.

The communities I passed through along the way have had a profound effect on me, one that I could never have anticipated in the hours and hours of detailed planning. I'm ready for the next adventure.

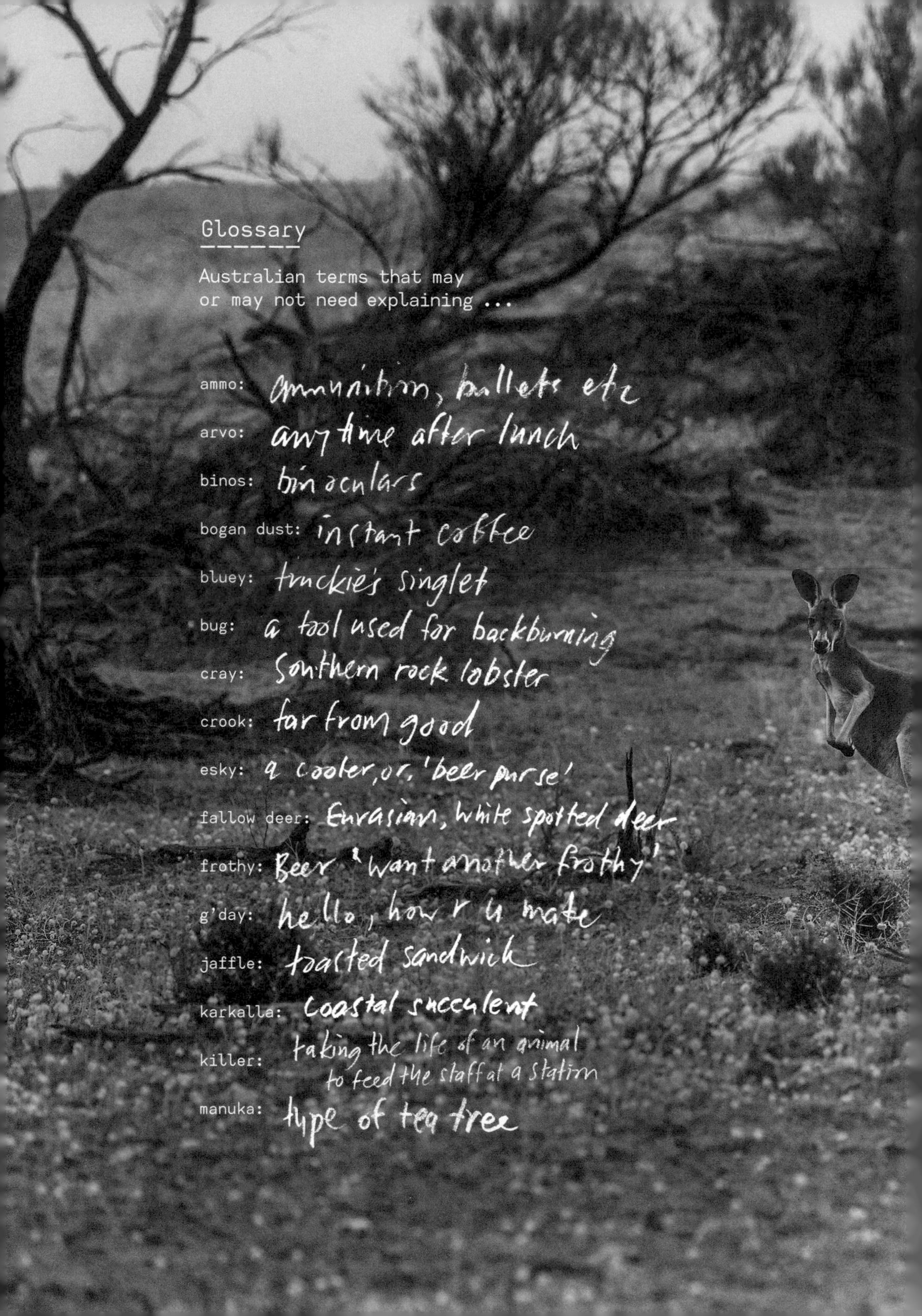

Glossary

Australian terms that may
or may not need explaining ...

ammo: ammunition, bullets etc

arvo: any time after lunch

binos: bin aculars

bogan dust: instant coffee

bluey: truckie's singlet

bug: a tool used for backburning

cray: Southern rock lobster

crook: far from good

esky: a cooler, or, 'beer purse'

fallow deer: Eurasian, white spotted deer

frothy: Beer "want another frothy"

g'day: hello, how r u mate

jaffle: toasted sandwich

karkalla: coastal succulent

killer: taking the life of an animal to feed the staff at a station

manuka: type of tea tree

mozzies: *mosquitoes*

muddies: *mudcrabs*

rip the scab off a cold one: *crack open a beer*

roo: *kangaroo*

saltbush: *Semi-arid native Australian shrub*

samphire: *native succulent*

sand rut: *sunken track or groove*

snatch strap: *for pulling a car out of mud*

schnitty: *Schnitzel*

servo: *Service station*

'Straya: *Australia*

stubbies: *Short workwear shorts*

swag: *Open air sleeping situation*

tassie: *Tasmania*

tinnie: *see frothy*

tinny: *small boat made from... tin*

wetty: *wetsuit, the thicker the better*

wheel skids: *traction pads to stop you getting bogged*

winnie blues: *winfield cigarettes*

Index

of people and places

Acknowledgements

This journey of discovery, a
selection of writings of this great
land, would not have been possible
without some wonderful people.
I want to thank them not only for
making it all happen, but also
for helping me and my team to grow.

Firstly, to my wife, Polly: Pol,
you're a rock, a beautiful, kind
and generous woman who inspires
me, grounds me and has supported
all my wild, spontaneous ideas over
the years. You've never clipped my
wings; your devotion to and love
of our two wild little ones, Harriet
and Henry, is something special to
witness; and to watch them grow with
purity and only the best ideals is
comforting.

To Nell, my rock at Biota, the one
who points me where I need to be:
Nell, your consummate organisational
skills, and your professionalism
in everything you do for all of us
is amazing, even if it does entail
taking rifles and ammo across
borders, on boats and planes...
If anybody can find a way to make
something happen, it's you, the
'get-shit-done girl'!

To Adam 'squid lips' Gibson: Gibbo,
mate, you go alright at the end of
the lens and you don't snore - a
real plus when you're living with a
bloke in the bush for a month or so.
Your drive and your passion for your
profession is infectious, and you're

talented yet down to earth (not a
wanker). You love the great outdoors
and we share the same respect for
the natural world. Can't wait
for the next instalment, big nuts!

Ryan 'loves a dart' Kovac: mate,
I can't begin to thank you for all
your support, company and advice,
for being a good listener and, at
times, for putting up with me. You
snore like a chaff-cutter and smoke
darts like a chimney, but apart
from that you're OK. Keep cooking
and loving nature, mate, and don't
settle for mediocre.

To JLR (Jaguar Land Rover Australia)
and James Scrimshaw, you and the
team at Spark 44 were so supportive
in making this trip a reality. The
Discovery you built for this trip
was bulletproof, a true testament
to the capability of these machines -
not only did the car get me from
A to B over some of the most hostile
roads and tracks in Australia, but
it gave me memories I will cherish
for the rest of my life.

Massive thanks to Jeanine and
Shannon of The Cru Media, as well
as Nicole Foster and her team at
Tourism Australia. Cheers for all
your help with getting a bunch of
disorganised chefs into some of the
most remote parts of the country.

Naomi, Natalia and the team at BLACK
Communications: without you guys

this trip would never have been thought of - you guys are awesome. I appreciate all your support, and I love working alongside such professionals.

To Wayne Hulme: Wayno, you bloody ripper. Your love for seafood and the people who catch it, and your loyalty, are amazing. Thank you for helping me organise this journey - it's taught me a lot about myself and about the country I love so much.

YETI Australia and Clayton Anderson are an epic force: thanks for all the cool gear (dad joke!), to which I'm now addicted. You can't have too many coolers and waterproof bags - you just never know what sort of adventure you're going to get caught up in, and if you find yourself stranded, a YETI 75 can fit 105 tinnies in it, so you'll have at least two days' worth of liquid to keep you hydrated...

To the team at Furneaux Freight, you were amazing in coordinating the shipping of our vehicle across to Flinders Island.

To Gulf Coast Agricultural Co., thank you from my team and me - you guys have always been huge supporters of our love of the land, and of our cooking. You are a constant source of inspiration. Over the years you have welcomed us with open arms - and you have always been so generous in sharing what station life means in rural Australia, giving me memories I will have forever. Thank you, guys.

To the entire Murdoch Books team, thank you for your patience and trust in this passionate project of mine. Justin Wolfers, thanks for the one on ones, and Corinne Roberts, thank you for the support and sound advice.

Also a big thanks to Tim West, Riley Aitken, Cameron Cansdell, the Bruce family, Ben Shephard and my parents - you all assisted in this expedition and made it possible.